A RETURN TO THE ASHES

Tara — thank you so much
for your support!

[signature]

A RETURN TO THE ASHES

NADINA POPOVICIU

NEW DEGREE PRESS

A RETURN TO THE ASHES

ISBN   978-1-63676-845-8   *Paperback*
        978-1-63730-197-5   *Kindle Ebook*
        978-1-63730-289-7   *Ebook*

Dedicated to my family, my ancestors, and Romania,
which will always hold a piece of my heart.

CONTENTS

AUTHOR'S NOTE

———

Growing up, I spent my free time either with my head in the clouds and music blasting in my ears or scribbling something down late at night. A lot of my inspiration came from the fantasy books I read growing up, and I took the time to experiment with my style—ranging from awful poetry to short stories—through high school. Yet ultimately, my studies began to take up the time I had originally dedicated to writing.

My family lives in Romania, and I visited them throughout my childhood. As I grew older, I enjoyed sitting in my grandparents' living rooms, listening to the stories of my family: how my grandparents met, how their parents met, what life was like in the countryside, and how it was to live during Romania's Communist era. I heard stories of how my grandfather couldn't go to college because he was a priest's son, and later how he was sent to a labor camp over less than a dollar's "waste of resources" in the military. I learned how my grandmother's parents met, and the early, unfortunate fates they suffered. I listened to how my other grandmother would wash her clothes or go to church in a small country village. I took it all in. My only regret is not listening as much or asking for more when I was younger.

The summer after I graduated high school, my parents drove my brother and me throughout our home region of Transylvania. We took winding roads through the Carpathians that would go through forest canopies, past small waterfalls and springs, and the occasional mountaintop views. We toured the stone fortresses and castles that peppered the Romanian country, walking through cobblestone roads that had existed since the Medieval era and possibly even before. We passed by various villages—some that had evolved with the times to look more like cities or suburbs and others that were still sparse with sheep in the field while dogs and cows roamed the unpaved roads.

During that trip, I had a compelling dream one night that I had been working as a spy for a *Game of Thrones* character. In the dream, I fell in love with a soldier who worked for the opposing side, and we had to figure out a way to escape from our lives. Upon waking up, I wrote down the idea and then started writing a short romance scene. I thought, *Hey, this would be a cool book idea!*

Not long after, we visited the Corvin Castle in Hunedoara. I distinctly recall a room I entered that looked like it came straight out of a *Game of Thrones* episode—a long room with tall, pointed arches and beveled columns lining the area. Excited, I took as many pictures as I could to use as inspiration for the story I had started writing. Those photos are still on my phone, and I used them to nail down the nitty-gritty details that bring my book to life and reference the culture and history of the country I left but never stopped loving.

Freshman year of college flew by, and I wrote a couple more scenes, but I got absorbed in my schoolwork and put it off. At the end of my Sophomore year, the COVID-19 pandemic hit. I headed home for an unknown period, along with many of my closest friends from high school. During quarantine, one of those friends called me up and asked if I wanted to try out *Dungeons & Dragons*. For the sake of trying something new and having an excuse to spend time with some of my favorite people, I agreed. I learned that an important part of the game is the character design process, including a character backstory. After writing that out, I decided to write a death scene for one of my character's old flames. I stayed up until three in the morning writing it and realized I could adapt that story for one of the characters in the book I'd been putting off for so long.

I decided to plunge myself back into my world of creativity. I spent a lot of time reading, both in and out of the fantasy genre. I also used ideas that I'd learned in my time as a Decision Science major at Carnegie Mellon, including psychological studies and behavioral science books I'd read for years before that.

I wanted to use these ideas to make the characters as relatable as possible but complex in their worldviews and backstories. Especially considering our hostile political climate that grows increasingly polarized by the day, I want the reader to identify with others, who they may not realize are vastly different from them, and to allow themselves to think outside of the views they've always had—whether a worldview or their self-perception.

More importantly, I wanted to underscore the values and themes that I think modern society has been failing to address—that no matter the sort of past someone has been through, they don't have the right to harm others. Nor does it make them right to base their decisions on the emotions they have experienced. I also wanted to show that just because one obtains the power to do something, justly or unjustly, doesn't mean that he or she should. The characters in this book purposefully have varying amounts and types of power to show how quickly and easily this dynamic can shift.

I was raised with the value that it was essential to educate myself and to think for myself. In this book, I want to empower women and men alike. I want to show that women can use their feminine side as a superpower rather than a weakness, as it is too often portrayed in the media, and that it comes with a responsibility to use it in a moral fashion. Likewise, men can view their masculinity as a force for good rather than something to play up or oppress, as either gender can and should find their ideal balance between the two in order to aspire to the highest level of morality that they can. I truly believe that when people define themselves in the extreme to any one side, it creates an imbalance within themselves and does more harm than good.

Most of all, I hope this book will take people on an engaging journey through the world I built. Books were my escape growing up, and I hope to provide my reader with an escape to another world that's both complex and fun, while giving them a piece of myself and the experiences and lessons I've had as a way to explore and question the real world around them.

FIFTEEN YEARS AGO

Sitting just outside their makeshift camp on the outskirts of the Marestran capital, the five-year-old girl fiddled with the pebbles she'd picked up as she looked over the cliff. She stared blankly into the waves that shuffled quietly below as the sun began to graze the edge of the horizon, its orange rays dancing across the sea. But the view, as lovely as it might have been to anyone else, did nothing to calm her.

Although she had been a few months on the road, and the visions no longer occupied every blink of her eye, they still haunted her dreams. Trying desperately to get into her home where she could hear her mother's piercing screams. The dark-haired boy lying there, his entire torso caught in the same purple flames that engulfed the village.

But the image of the balaur was the hardest to ignore. The massive creature was like nothing she'd ever seen before: with feet that crushed grown men like bugs, batlike wings that cast a shadow over the entire street, and seven heads— one of which looked directly at her. She didn't think she'd ever forget the glowing eyes, the drool that hardened into crystals when dripping out of its mouth, the razor-sharp teeth—bigger than her—that it bared as its long neck snaked around the building. When it opened its mouth, a lavender glow inside grew bigger and bigger until it formed a stream of fire that she just barely escaped. But not without the fire searing her upper back and the crystals scraping across it as her shouts joined the chorus of chaos that had become of her peaceful little village in the mountains. That was the most excruciating pain she'd ever felt.

Whenever she had time to herself, those screams echoed in her mind, despite the fact that she was hundreds of miles from the ruins she'd called home not too long ago.

Not hearing the footsteps nearby, she gasped as she heard, "Citrina," and felt a gentle hand on her back. Even though the burns had healed, she still preferred to forget about them, avoiding mirrors and touch alike. After all, who'd want to see such a thing? The tight, dark-purple skin was laced with milky-white scratches across it. None of the healers they talked to had ever seen such a thing. And though Citrina didn't like people seeing her back, it was the only way their small group of survivors could get *anyone* to believe their story as they traveled from kingdom to kingdom, searching for a new home.

Looking up, her eyes met with warm brown ones. Lumina was an old friend of her parents' who had saved her from the fire and treated her like her own daughter. At this point, she might as well have been. Her parents hadn't been lucky enough to survive, if anyone could even call it "lucky."

"What did they say?" Citrina asked hopefully, crawling to sit in Lumina's lap.

Lumina grimaced. "The good news is they believed us. Said they'd heard of sightings in the northwest a couple of months back and sent men to take care of it."

Citrina sat up straight, giving the woman an incredulous look. "Th-they killed it?"

She shrugged. "So they claim."

"So, we're safe!"

Lumina's eyes turned sad, and she took a deep breath with a halfhearted smile. "From the monster, yes."

"Shouldn't we celebrate then? What're we waiting for?"

The woman brushed some of Citrina's hair behind one ear, hesitating for a moment before continuing. "The Marestran King claims they've done enough good for us. That we ought to figure things out for ourselves instead of relying on them for help."

The young girl's eyes widened. "So..."

"Another rejection."

Tears filled Citrina's eyes. They'd have to keep moving, but where could they go? Every other place had kicked them out. She'd heard Marestra had a strong force and knew they didn't have much time to stay in the country.

"What's gonna happen to us, Lumina?" She couldn't stop the tremor in her voice.

The woman wrapped her arms around Citrina, holding her tightly and smoothing out her hair. "We'll figure it out. We'll be stronger than them. They'll learn their lesson. We'll make sure of it."

ONE

JASPER

Jasper's eyes narrowed as he drew the arrow back, the fletching tickling his cheek as his grip remained tight on the curve of the bow. The late afternoon sun now hid behind the trees, and the air was still in this grassy, shaded area between the forest and the soldiers' quarters. Trees towered over one side and three stories of stone stood on the other. No one would bother him here. The conditions were perfect.

Breathing slowly, Jasper released the arrow with his right hand, and he watched it dart sixty feet ahead of him, seemingly hitting the target right in the middle. As he walked over to investigate, he noticed that he'd just barely missed the painted middle dot. "Fuck," he whispered under his breath.

"Are you tired or just getting old?" Out of the corner of his eye, a tall blond figure appeared. He turned to see his stepbrother Anghel leaning against the nearby wall on the outside of the soldiers' quarters, his arms crossed with a smirk on his face.

Rolling his eyes, Jasper pulled the arrow out of the hay and began walking back to his original spot, the grass brushing his ankles. "You know archery is my weak point."

"You don't have to be so hard on yourself. That shot still would have killed a man."

"Perhaps, but it could be the difference between a mortal wound and a finishing strike. I think it worse to leave a man to bleed to death. I need that kind of precision if I am to be of any good in your service."

Anghel snorted. "If you were not, my father would not have made you Lieutenant, and at twenty-one, no less. You *are* the best of us."

"You flatter me in saying so, brother, but the role requires maintenance and perfection. I can't afford to slip up."

"You could use that energy to train the other soldiers to be as good as you."

"It's all I do in training," Jasper breathed, positioning his feet and drawing back another arrow, his focus narrowing on the painted stack of hay ahead. "It's why I have to rely on my spare time to train for myself at all." Releasing the arrow, he landed it in the middle of the target again and walked back over to assess his work.

His brother sighed. "You really only ever train and eat and sleep. You need a life outside of this too." Anghel motioned with his head to the door of the soldiers' quarters, the border between Jasper's peaceful training space and the rest of the city soldiers who relied on him. "Some of the boys and I are going to the Maiden's Mug tonight. You're not on watch, so you have no excuse *not* to join us."

"But I have to—"

"Bullshit," Anghel said, walking over and throwing his hands up. "We're in peacetime. Gods, do something else for a change. When's the last time you had a woman?"

Jasper felt the heat rise to his cheeks. "That's none of your concern."

"As your brother and best friend, it *is* my concern, and the fact that you get so defensive tells me the answer is 'too long.' We are changing that tonight." His brother grabbed him by the arm and pulled him, but Jasper fought it. Anghel stopped for a moment, his light lavender eyes looking at Jasper intently.

"As your Prince," he continued, "I hereby *order* you to join me at this tavern."

Jasper rolled his eyes, picking up the hay target and following his brother through the door to the soldiers' quarters. "Had to pull the royal authority card, did you?" he muttered.

The Prince chuckled. "Left me with no choice."

As the men walked into the tavern, a wave of sound flooded their ears: music played by half-talented bards, women pretending to laugh at the jokes of men with gold in their pockets, mugs slapping on tables as drunken commoners, men and women alike, sang along to the jigs.

The four men—Jasper, Anghel, and two Sergeants, Tarren and Osbert—made their way to the back, where a table had been cleared for them. The Prince frequented the Maiden's Mug so often that this table was specially reserved for his convenience, and the commoners had gotten used to his presence. Anghel and his men always considered it comforting to have a place to escape from the formalities of the castle and the smell of the soldiers' quarters while still being treated to good drinks.

Ales had already been placed for the four of them, and the party didn't hesitate to sit and start sharing jokes and stories as usual. Jasper even found himself smiling. Perhaps this little break wasn't so bad. If anything, it was nice.

Until women came into the discussion.

"What about that one?" Anghel asked, gesturing toward a woman who passed by, but Jasper was the only one who didn't bother to look. It felt juvenile to him.

The Prince scoffed, disappointed. "What's the point of finding women for you if you don't even look at them?"

"Some of us prefer to focus on our duties," Jasper retorted, slapping a hand on his brother's back. "I'm just here to have a drink with some good men and go home."

"*Some of us prefer to focus on our duties,*" his brother mocked. "You're such a joy-killer."

"You can still go home, and just take 'er," Tarren pointed out, motioning with his dark-stubbled chin.

Jasper still didn't bother to look. "No."

"What about 'er?" Osbert offered, subtly pointing a bony finger at another one.

Looking at the skinny, red-haired Sergeant, Jasper replied, "Why don't *you* have her?"

Anghel looked at his brother with a pitying expression. "At the very least just *look* around. Give these poor girls a chance. It's not like you're a fucking monk."

"Whores are *your* specialty, not mine," Jasper countered with a sip of his ale before placing his head down on the table, the fatigue from the day of training in the sun finally catching up with him. Just as his eyes closed, he felt a flick on the back of his head and slowly sat back up.

"'Aven't 'ad 'nough drinks for that, good sir," said Osbert, a mischievous grin lighting up his wolfish, freckled face.

"And we're not letting you off easy 'til you find *someone* for the night. Have a bit of fun, Lieutenant," added Tarren, running a beefy, callused hand through his own scruffy dark hair before taking another swig.

Jasper sighed. "Why?" he asked, irked.

"Wha', d'ya have an issue get'n it up? 'Cause the 'pothecary helped me a lot wi' that," his large friend whispered, a bit too loud for the table.

"I do not."

"You like men?" Osbert asked. Quickly, he added, "No' a problem, just makes grapplin' a lil' more awkward."

"I like women, alright? And I can exercise whatever part of me *whenever* I want to."

"Sure doesn't seem like it," Anghel commented, finishing his drink and twice-tapping the bottom of the mug on the table for a refill that came soon after. "Can't imagine why you'd be so opposed otherwise."

"I just prefer my women… how can I put it nicely… not bought to please me," Jasper told them, "nor sleeping with me just so they can say they fucked someone of status."

The men laughed. "Lookin' f'r a unicorn," Tarren commented.

The Lieutenant shrugged. "Then so be it."

Anghel turned his body toward his brother, his legs on either side of the bench, and his eyes freezing the Lieutenant into place. "You're going to die alone acting like that, you know, while the rest of us find women and eventually get tied down. If you don't go out and at least *try* your hand at a few, you'll never find one you even like. Especially when you spend all your time holed up in the soldiers' yard." He scoffed, drinking from his ale. "And we know women aren't brought there for training."

Jasper glared at his brother. He knew Anghel had a point. After a few seconds of intense eye contact, he broke with a sigh, deciding to humor the Prince. "Fine."

Glancing around the room, through a sea of scantily clad women looking to make a buck or start a rumor, he found his gaze landing on one woman. She wore a dark headscarf, unusual for women here, but her eyes kept him staring. Even from across the room, he saw that they seemed to have a mischievous glint in them, lighting up her porcelain face and soft, yet striking, features that appeared just as delicate. Only a second must have passed before she turned around and vanished.

When Jasper looked back at his friends, he was met with plastered smirks and a small chorus of, "See?" and, "There we go!"

"You found one, didn't you?" Anghel asked, trying to follow where he'd been looking. "Where is she?"

Hesitating, the Lieutenant landed his eyes on another woman, this one with auburn hair and dark-green-colored eyelids. Her face was average-looking, but the features beneath it were put on display. Her supple, most personal parts were just barely covered by green clothing—the trademark dress for a Padaurean prostitute.

"The one in green," he decided. Their eyes met, and he winked, beckoning her over.

"Alright, brother, well done! Told you that you could be a charmer!" Anghel applauded, while Jasper stayed cool with another sip of his drink.

As the woman approached their table with her chest puffed out, Jasper leaned toward her and brought her in with a palm on the small of her back, slipping a gold coin into her hand and whispering into her ear. He could feel the men's eyes on them in anticipation, as if they were prepubescent boys trying to sneak a peek of a woman at the baths.

Pulling away, he watched the smirk on Osbert's face turn to one of surprise as the woman moved to straddle the farmer's boy. Standing up, Jasper made sure to wink at the other men before leaving the prostitute with them and making his way to the bar.

Jasper made eye contact with the barman as he approached, signaling for one more ale. The barman nodded, first handing the drink he'd already poured to a woman by Jasper's side before getting one for him. With the sound of the beverage flowing into the cup faint among the chatter and noise in the tavern, the Lieutenant turned to survey the room. Then his eyes fell on the woman beside him who was doing the same, watching those around them as if it were a play put on just for them.

The dark blue headscarf was loosely draped over her head, and her dress, of the same color, was of a more efficient and comfortable fashion than that of the ladies who normally frequented this tavern. Not to mention it was more conservative, although it hugged her form enough to still show the curves of her slender body. Despite the strange dress, she seemed to sit unnoticed by most. After all, who would look at cloth over skin?

Only when she turned did he realize he'd been staring, and her large, dark eyes met his. Her smooth skin momentarily flushed, but other than that she betrayed no diffidence. Rather, one of her eyebrows arched apprehensively. Jasper, abashed, suddenly focused on swirling the ale in his cup and looking at that, though from the corner of his eye, he still watched her fluid movements as she gracefully sipped from her own drink and, might he even say, chuckled?

After taking another sip, he turned, perplexed by her calm, humble demeanor that contrasted so wildly with their environment, and found it in himself to ask, "You're not from around here, are you?" Right as he said that, he mentally kicked himself for being so blunt, especially with—from what he could tell by the way she carried herself—a lady, even if a foreign one.

She didn't seem to notice, or at the very least, didn't seem to care about that. A little smirk painted her face as she turned back to him, silent for a moment before turning back to face the room. "I can only imagine what gave it away," she replied, placing her cup on the countertop. "I'm afraid I don't frequent these establishments too often." The young lady began to reach within a fold of her dress, but Jasper was the first to brandish a coin.

"If I pay for that drink of yours, would you walk with me outside and tell me how you came to be here, then?"

Her smile grew, and her gaze momentarily dropped down to her lap before she looked back up, her cheeks rosy again. "I take it this sort of place isn't to your particular liking either, is it?"

Jasper looked back at Anghel and the two other men, with the woman still in his friend's lap and raucous laughter erupting from the group. "You could say that," he confessed, turning back to her and betraying a small grin in return. Maybe his brother *had* taught him a thing or two.

Placing the coin on the countertop, he thanked the barman before walking out of the tavern with the lady, her pace so light that she seemed to float through the room.

The cobblestone streets were dimly lit by the light of a sun that had just dipped below the horizon, their shadows stretching over the empty streets. They walked by small buildings filled with people either drinking with friends or home after a long day at work. A quiet hum of voices and laughter emitted from the insides of the clay houses they passed, but otherwise, it was a tranquil atmosphere, which

Jasper had always preferred to the noise and chatter that he dealt with throughout the day.

He idly looked around as they walked, the words now coming to him with more ease. "So what brings you over to the Padaurean Capital?"

The woman smiled a little. "I've been traveling. Nothing too interesting, I'm afraid." Now that he could hear her more clearly, her voice seemed to have a hint of an accent, but from where, he couldn't tell.

"I would bargain that any place you've been would be more interesting."

She laughed hollowly along with him, a faraway look in her eyes that she shook off as quickly as it had appeared. It seemed she didn't want to be pushed to talk much about that.

He continued, "B-but my guess is that, for anyone, at least, a new place is more interesting than home."

"You could say that," she agreed, "but for some, 'home' is a word that warrants more trouble than it's worth." Looking around, she pivoted to another subject before he had the chance to ask her anything about what she meant. "Have you always lived here?"

"Almost my entire life," Jasper told her, combing his hair with his fingers. "Although I couldn't say I remember much of my life before coming here."

"So I assume you must have a trade by now," she replied.

He chuckled. "You could say that. The King, in his good graces, adopted me when I was very young and raised me alongside his own son. Now I've been trained and given command of the city's Royal Guard."

"Wow," she said, her eyebrows raised. "And forgive me for saying so, but you seem quite young for that position. You must be a remarkable soldier."

Jasper felt the heat rise to his cheeks. "It's very kind of you to say, my lady."

The light in her eyes made his heart skip a beat. "More honest than kind, I would think."

He looked away, hoping his cheeks weren't too red.

She continued, "You don't have any duties to get to tonight? I would think you have more important things to do than wander around town with a stranger."

The Lieutenant shook his head. "Tonight is one of my few nights off." The night's darkness had started to creep in through the alleys, adding a contrast to the light that poured out from the windows of the inns and homes around them.

Their silence continued, and he looked over only to meet her eyes. Swallowing, he found it in himself to speak up again, despite his heart hammering and his conscience calling him an idiot for not being more interesting. "Speaking of which, it seems to be getting dark out, and I should be getting back. Would you care to join me for wine at the castle?" He motioned toward the castle that overlooked the city with his arm held out for her to take.

Her smile turned small and coy. "I am not one to join strange men for wine, especially if I don't know their names."

As soon as she'd pointed it out, he realized to his embarrassment that he'd completely forgotten to ask her for her name, and he hoped he didn't look too flustered as he told her, "Mine is Jasper. I would love to know yours and if perhaps that changes anything."

She laughed, pausing before she took his arm. "Perhaps this time, it does. And they call me Onyx."

The castle's red rooftops seemed to disappear into the darkness of the night sky, but the torches along the bridge to the entrance illuminated their path as the conversation continued, passing by the guards who parted for them. She looked around with interest, observing the internal courtyard as he led her up the stairs to his chambers.

He welcomed her, opening the door for her and trying not to show his mild abashment at the sparse arrangement of the room. There wasn't much to decorate it outside of the bed and bedside tables, but she didn't seem to mind in the slightest. If anything, she seemed to feel right at home, walking to the window by the bed to look out at the view of the city. Jasper stayed by the door as one of the servants fetched him wine in two chalices. Bringing over the beverages, he joined her at the window, handing one of the drinks to her as he sat down on the bed, and she followed suit.

She thanked him, and her eyes returned to the city. "I imagine this view is hard to get used to," she said softly. "Just thinking about how many lives fill it, how many people are out there laughing and spending time with their families, each with their own worries and pleasures."

He followed her gaze and started to see a sort of life that seemed to fill the city—one he hadn't really taken the time to notice before. Most nights he was either occupied with training or watch. Or, as the only sober one, dragging his brother out of trouble.

"To my shame, I hadn't ever thought about it," he admitted, taking a sip of his wine and then placing the chalice on the windowsill. "Yet now that you mention it, the idea does bring a new sort of light to it. I think it's a nice reminder of why I do... what I do."

Jasper looked back at Onyx, who took a sip as well and placed her chalice next to his before looking back up at him. In the light and this proximity, he noticed so much more about her. Her eyes were an entrancing dark gray, and her headscarf had fallen to her shoulders to reveal dark honey-colored hair that seemed to shine like bronze in the candlelight. She smelled like the breeze through a linden tree as she smiled for a second and then shyly looked down at her lap, her cheeks flushing red again.

As if it were a habit of something that possessed him, his hand reached to brush her hair behind her ear and then traced down below her chin, tilting her face up to bring her incredibly tender lips to his. Jasper's veins felt like they were filling up with a sort of energy he'd never felt before. His arms snaked around her waist, and Onyx moved along as if in the same rhythm with him. She swung her leg over as she moved to straddle him, her fingers running through his dark hair while she pressed her body against his.

Her hands continued to travel, going down only to come back up under his shirt and help him remove it. Slowly but surely, she removed her scarf entirely to expose silky hair that fell to her hips, and he swiveled her around, pinning her to the bed. She seemed to welcome him, her arms snaking around to pull him closer as his hands continued to explore her body, gingerly trailing under her dress.

TWO

CITRINA

———

Citrina watched the slow rise and fall of her lover's chest, listening for variations in his breathing. She deftly shifted from beneath the covers and onto all fours on the floor, careful not to shake the bed or cause any sound before standing up. Now that she knew he was a high-ranking officer, there was no such thing as too careful. If he really was that good, even the subtle squeak of a mouse might be enough to wake him.

She took a moment to observe him, especially those tender lips that parted slightly and that dark, wavy hair that hung over closed lids, recalling those stunning hazel eyes of his. Most of his tall, refined figure was concealed by the sheets, and even his arms were covered by fine silk wraps that he hadn't taken off. Perhaps it was an element of the culture here, and that would be all the more to her luck.

The scout wasn't one to believe in luck itself, but she was tempted to when faced with the coincidence that one of the most handsome men she'd ever laid eyes on was in a powerful position close to the Padaurean royal family, not to mention kind and understanding. He hadn't necessarily been the best she'd had, but he was decent. And something was different about him, compared to the other men she'd used for information.

Shaking her head, she tried to push out of her mind the strange energy she had felt in Jasper's arms, with his lips on hers. Even if he had any reason to remember her the next day, he'd only know her by Onyx—one of the several aliases she used to protect her identity during her scouting missions.

Within the shadows of the room and slivers of moonlight cracking through the curtains, she dressed herself. Looking down, she realized the wrap on her own forearm had shifted, barely revealing the brand of a phoenix just below her left elbow with a few of the tallies beside it. She hoped Jasper hadn't seen it. After all, he didn't say anything about it and didn't seem to be paying much attention to her arms, of all her features. He hadn't even taken off her dress entirely, and all for the better. She didn't have to explain her scars. Breathing out a soft sigh of relief at that notion, she rolled the wrap back over the branding, remembering the advice of her leader.

Men are visual creatures, Lumina had said. *They think it to be a strength, that what they see and have seen makes them all the wiser. That's what makes women so potentially dangerous, my child.*

The words continued to resonate through Citrina's mind as she quietly fled from the room, listening intently for any sound that might break the stiff silence filling the castle. *We entice their eyes and consume their grasp, and what do they have left?*

She breezed through the dark, empty corridors, her eyes flitting between the large arches on her left that exposed the barren courtyard below and the stone walls to her right that were peppered with doors to locked chambers. *In that moment, they cede all power and control to us as their momentary pleasure. Where is their wisdom then?*

One door, however, had its lock just barely loose. Placing her ear by the crack, Citrina could not detect a single sound. Reaching into one of her hidden pockets, she felt around for her largest stone, a honey-colored crystal the size of her thumb—citrine, her namesake, a stone that she had grown to love along with the scars that had given her a unique ability. She ran her fingers over the tip and took a deep breath, pulling the energy out of the stone to hone her vision and her hearing. As it softly glowed, she could hear even the mice running in the dungeon and the snores of various people in the castle. Now she knew for sure no one was in the room as not a single breath came from that area.

Slowly, she pushed the door a little. It moved slightly but did not open. She pushed against it again, this time a little harder, hoping not to make any sort of sound. A creak ensued, and her heart sped up. Looking around again, she still saw nothing moving behind her or below her in the courtyard, miraculously. Not a single shadow shifted, and she heard no stirring of any sort. It *was* the dead of night, and with the exception of the night's watchmen, not a soul in their right mind would be awake right now.

Slipping in, she found a desk near the window with letters that had been left out, some, it seemed, for the ink to dry. Others simply had been strewn about messily. She didn't dare touch them, lest someone notice that something was off. But she read them all, every black trace on the fine parchment, taking care to memorize the information before she returned to the corridors, gingerly closing the door and leaving it in the same position she'd found it.

Flitting through several castle floors, she memorized the layout—where the chamber doors were, the defense towers with half-asleep soldiers on watch, the balcony that stood over the soldiers' quarters just outside the castle, the winding staircases that swirled into the dungeons.

Eventually, she found her way into the cellars, hearing the faint moaning of a prisoner in one direction and the distant call of an owl in the other. She elected to follow the sound of the latter, traveling into a darkness that was hard to see in even with her enhanced vision.

The hair rose on the back of her neck, but she continued, each careful step seeming to drag on. She heard a faint cicada's buzzing, getting progressively louder until she found a small hole in a corner only about two feet tall, just barely illuminating this hidden part of the depths with the moonlight that seeped in. After electing to crawl through it, Citrina found herself at the bottom of a small hill that was covered with trees, the castle towering above her and the outskirts of the city almost out of her line of sight. The building was at once a magnificent and intimidating sight, and she could imagine that most Padaureans dared not come too close.

Taking a deep breath, she turned and disappeared into the trees, sneaking through the forest. As she began her trek back to the base in the heart of the mountain range, she repeated softly to herself the information she had read in the letters, careful not to forget anything. She was excited to share with Lumina both the new information and what their informants had told them to expect all along.

We can be the first to take full advantage of that before they even realize what they've done to themselves.

THREE

LETTA

Sitting down on a bench, Letta looked around the garden, memorizing the sight of the flowers that had just begun to open up, their petals lit only by the half-moon in the sky. They looked less delicate now, with their petals drained of their color by the darkness. She preferred it that way, anyway. After all, they were just a pretty thing to observe during the day and nothing more.

Still, she knew she would miss this small garden, the place where she would sneak out and stroll in the night, when the philosophical ramblings in her head grew too loud and she needed a place larger than her chambers to breathe them out.

The night has a way of doing that, enticing people with overwhelming thoughts, fantasies that go beyond daytime activities. Perhaps it's why people sleep in the night. They can not—or do not want to—handle that.

She, however, was up to the challenge. Her mind was always somewhere else, a trait both she and her younger sister had inherited from their mother. Although those two preferred to daydream about unrealistic Princes and fields of flowers. They didn't share her curiosity for the way the world actually was, ugliness hand-in-hand with beauty.

Shame, that we use frivolous things to distract us from reality. Am I cursed with the company of only these *people for the rest of my life?* She sighed. *At least I'll be taking my books.*

"I figured I would find you out here." Letta turned to see a temporary burst of light as her mother stepped out into the garden and shut the door to their castle. The daughter shrugged and turned to watch the moon, ignoring her mother to wonder what it saw beyond the tall bushes that blocked their view of the surrounding world.

Despite her daughter's silence, the Duchess moved gracefully to Letta's side. "Rumor has it the Apasian Castle has a grand garden, one that makes this one look like a mud pile. I imagine you must be excited about that."

Letta nodded silently, not wanting to admit she hadn't been listening when hearing about the places her father had traveled. It all sounded like boring court gossip and politics to tune out, so she had no idea what awaited her.

"Apparently, a nice library too."

"I hope they use it."

"That is no way to talk about your future family."

"Am I wrong? Most of the royals that Tata is friends with are total bores, the women and men all talking about who-said-what and not much else. I imagine even in wartime it'd be boring."

Her mother glanced at her sharply and then chuckled to herself. "There *is* a good bit of gossip, I will give you that. But there is more to our responsibilities. Even those who don't have their noses stuck in a book have important things to say."

"I doubt anything interesting."

"You might be surprised. You say this now, but you will only realize one day that pure intellect in itself has no charm."

She gently brushed a lock of Letta's hair out of her face. "It's why seduction doesn't happen in a study room."

"Yet for any man who sets eyes on a woman with an active mind, it's fatal to lack wit, no matter his charm," Letta replied, wondering if her mother got the reference to the book she'd just finished herself.

"That's true, and I pray that your future husband is well-endowed in that respect. Fate bringing together a simpleton with someone like you would be playing a sick joke. He would be cluelessly entranced by your beauty, and the poor man would be picked apart for the rest of his life."

"Mama!"

"What? I cannot be honest with my daughter?" The Duchess laughed.

Letta sputtered, flustered. "That's—"

"Can you trust your father?" her mother continued. "He has met the family before, and I have faith that he made the decision thoughtfully. Alliance of Padaure with the Apasians wasn't his only motive. He could have sent you to be married off to our Prince, but both he and the King deemed the young man too immature for you."

She had a point. The Duke was meticulous with every single detail and decision he came across. If he put half as much thought into her marriage as he did into the arrangement of food on his plate, perhaps it wasn't so hopeless after all.

"Has he met my betrothed?" Letta asked, hoping not to sound too eager.

"He said only briefly. Apparently, your Prince spends a lot of time in the library or outside."

"Oh?" Letta raised an eyebrow. Maybe she could be all right with him.

"Does that make you feel better?"

Letta crossed her arms, watching the moon as well as the gray clouds dancing around and over it. "Perhaps." She felt a kiss on her forehead before the Duchess began to walk back inside.

The woman turned around one more time as she opened the door to the castle, her thick, dark-brown hair shuffling around her shoulders. "You will *love* it there. I know it."

Maybe she would.

"I can't believe you're actually getting married!" Atora squealed, rushing to embrace Letta, who gingerly hugged her back and patted her on the head. She could hardly believe she was going to be a wife soon and that her little sister was almost of age as well. Atora was sixteen, only one year younger, yet Letta still felt like the girl was just a child, too naïve and innocent to deal with courts. Although in reality, her charm probably better suited her for that than Letta's did.

"It's good news for you as well. That means Tata's probably looking for a husband for you too."

The younger sister jumped on the bed, causing the packed bags to bounce a little. Letta rearranged them to make sure nothing was messed up before tying the bags closed.

"I hope I get to marry a Prince too." The thick brown hair Atora had gotten from Mama spread out all over the place as she basked in the rays of dawn that peeked through the window.

Letta rolled her eyes. Of course, she did. She'd spent her entire life with her nose in books of romance and fairytales. "I'm sure Tata would love that as well." She sighed.

"And we'll visit each other! Or write letters!" Atora squeaked excitedly.

The older sister nodded to appease her. "Certainly." Closing the last bag, Letta turned to see Atora looking at her with tears welling up in her eyes. She felt her throat tighten as she tried to hold back her own tears, realizing how much both of them had grown up from the two little girls getting in trouble for playing in the fountain. Now they were two bookworms whose interests had created a bit of distance between them, especially regarding the level of intellect that had developed differently for the sisters.

Turning around to compose herself, Letta found herself staring at an empty bookshelf, swallowing as her gaze fell on one last book she hadn't been able to bring herself to pack: *The Ancient School of Love and War*. Picking it up, her fingers delicately brushed the worn cover and parchment that she had turned over countless times. It had been one of her greatest reads, by far.

Letta looked back at her sister, thinking it may not be too late for her. "I want you to have this," she said, extending the book out.

The girl looked at her incredulously, reaching out a hand but sharply pulling it back. "But it's your favorite book. I couldn't."

I didn't realize she paid attention. Letta smiled. "I've read it enough to get the gist. Besides, I think you might like it. Maybe it'd be one of the few things we can share. And whenever you *are* able to visit me, we can talk about it."

Atora rushed to hug her one last time. "Thank you," she whispered.

The older girl fully embraced her this time, taking in the feeling of her sister in her arms, the sweet flowery scent and soft brown hair that Atora always spent too long brushing. This was it. This was the last time she'd see her before the wedding, and after that, for who knew how long?

The servants came in to take her bags down and she followed them to the carriage—a four-wheeled, box-shaped black car decorated with intricate light blue designs and a scripted "A" alongside the blackbird sigil of their kingdom—pulled by two dark-brown horses. Letta hugged her parents only quickly enough to not feel herself tear up. Otherwise, she would start to cry.

She took in the moment as she stepped back. Her mother's light-gray eyes welled up with tears as her father restlessly scratched his silver-peppered scarlet beard while he directed her with unsolicited advice. Her sister sniffled and constantly tried to get in one last hug. Nodding constantly, Letta reassured them that yes, she would write them, and yes, she would be polite and remember her manners and make a good impression on her future husband and his family.

When the carriage door finally closed, she was met with her favorite servant, Col, the one who knew of her fondness for the quiet. He sat up straight, arranging his dark-brown hair, but said nothing as she rearranged her long silk dress to sit more comfortably, simply nodding to acknowledge her as the horses trotted off. Her family waved at her as the car moved away in the dawning sun. Once they were out of sight, she welcomed the pleasant silence, opening a book and bracing herself for the long trip, anxious yet excited for what was to come.

FOUR

––––––

"You shouldn't be doing that," she told Petyr.

He sat beside her in the alley, relaxed in their apparent invisibility from the townspeople as he took a bite of the bread he had just picked off a cart. "If the person you stole from doesn't realize anything's gone, you know they don't need it all that much."

She scoffed, rolling her eyes. "Doesn't make it right."

"But it makes it a bit more justified. Besides, just the right amount of wrong makes it more fun." He winked and offered the bread to her. She was hungry—after all, she was at least as skinny as he was—and she began to reach out hesitantly before drawing her hand back.

He chuckled and tore a piece off, placing it in her hands. "It's not poisoned, at least as far as I know," he joked.

She betrayed a small smile, taking a bite. The bread was warm and so soft that she felt as though she had bitten into a cloud. The sixteen-year-old girl hadn't tasted such fresh bread in weeks.

"And if it makes you feel better, the more we eat, the less they have, which is also nice."

The girl gasped, looking around to make sure no one had heard them. All the townsfolk had their fair share of disdain for the lords of their village—the "royals," as the commonfolk called them—especially for the lord's son, a man who would prance around town with a puffed chest, sneering at children and skinning alive the occasional animal he could get his hands on. But it was still taboo for anyone to say it so openly.

She grabbed him by the arm and pulled him close, scolding him in a hushed tone. "You shouldn't be saying things like that out loud, you know. You're going to get yourself killed."

His eyes immobilized the girl, a beautiful shade of honey illuminated by the occasional shards of sunlight that leaked through the dust in the air and the edges of the straw roofs above them. Her heart hammered in her chest as he moved closer so his lips were just inches from hers and then moved to whisper into her ear as he brushed back a strand of her blond hair. His hand faintly brushed up her arm, leaving a tingle on her skin wherever he touched.

"It's exciting to do what you shouldn't every once in a while. Isn't it?"

Her cheeks flushed, and she wasn't quite sure what to say. She just kept looking at him, her mouth empty of the words she could say, knowing that anything involving him would be trouble. But the idea intrigued her, nonetheless.

Petyr pulled back, that grin still on his face as he looked around the alley. "What would I have to do to court a fair lady? Jump on the roofs? Bring her a kitten?" His eyes lit up. "No... I'll find something proper for her to wear. It's not fair that the royals get all the luxury while we sit here in rags."

She snorted. "And in what world could you get something like that?"

He grinned. "Anything I can swipe, I can afford."

"Even if you could, they'd kill you for trying."

"And if by chance, they don't?"

She didn't have an answer.

"Ah, forget it." They turned back to face the slice of the town square in their view, watching the townspeople mill around. The merchants called over anyone with a coin as children ran through the shifting forest of legs. "But if I asked a certain maiden to meet me by the mill tomorrow at dusk, do you believe she would?"

She tried to hide her grin. "I don't see why not."

FIVE

OTRA

———

To celebrate her Marestran scouting mission coming to a close, Otra decided she wanted to stop by a tavern in the area. It was late, but she hoped not too late for her to grab a drink. Walking past an inn, she saw the innkeeper looking hesitantly at a man dressed in purple robes. Based on the styling, the man couldn't have been a royal. The robes were not intricately designed enough, and Marestran royals thought it low of them to stoop to commoners' ranks by visiting the local inns and taverns. But he was for sure a judge of some sort.

As she approached the entrance, she noticed a girl with mousy brown hair, who couldn't have been older than twelve, tensed up and looking uncomfortable—on the verge of tears, even—with no one else in the lobby. The three of them didn't notice her at first upon her entrance, and she was able to catch some of the conversation.

"She seems a bit young for you, sir…"

"The younger ones are better," replied the judge, no younger than fifty, stroking the girl's hair and making her tense up even more. "You wouldn't refuse an administrator now, would you?"

The innkeeper seemed to finally notice Otra's presence as she sat down on a stool beside them, dryly offering her the specials for the night. Nodding, she ordered an ale and looked over.

The woman's gut twisted. The girl wasn't much older than she had been when men started noticing her body, before Lumina and the Phoenix had found her and learned of her talents. A shame that the demand hadn't changed much in the past ten years.

"You know, I'm younger than I look," Otra whispered, leaning in as the girl's father poured her drink, "*and* a virgin. I could take him off both your hands for a little while."

The innkeeper looked at her, eyes wide in what appeared to be a mix of shock and hope. Swallowing, he handed her the drink and leaned into the official to relay the information. Otra felt the man's eyes trailing over her and just barely caught his sigh with, "I suppose she'll do for the night."

The official strolled past them and leaned into her, the stench of beer and bad breath filling up her nostrils as he gave her the directions to his room in the inn and directed her to be there within a quarter-hour's time. She nodded obediently, and finally, he walked out.

Looking over, she saw the innkeeper embracing the girl who shared his eyes and cheekbones, gently kissing her forehead. When their eyes met, she could see his own had tears welled up, and he mouthed a *thank you* to her. Nodding, she finished her drink and adjusted her neckline to expose more of her chest as she walked out of the room.

Her dark red dress hugged her figure as her long, dark curls tickled the top of her bare back. She arrived at a certain door and knocked on it gently, composing herself and hoping that a thirty-year age difference was enough for him.

Her newfound client, the gray-haired judge, opened the door, taking in the shape of her figure before looking back up at her face. She gave him a small smile, knowing her green eyes often entranced the men, especially in contrast to the color of that dress. The man motioned for her to enter, and she shyly complied.

"Are you a virgin like he told me?" he asked, shutting the door and wasting no time in removing his shirt to expose a white-haired chest and swollen gut. He looked her up and down as he walked around her. He was rather short for a man, she noticed, not much taller than her. Looking back at him, she nodded slowly and innocently. Men were often willing to pay more for virgins like her, and this free offer, combined with her looks, would make her an irresistible choice for any man who wasn't a eunuch.

He grinned, walking over and greedily massaging her breasts with one hand from behind her—first on top of her dress and then underneath. Closing her eyes, she took a moment to enjoy the touch and slipped off the top half of her dress to reveal her chest, glad that he didn't notice, or at least didn't care, about the white scars that patterned her tan torso. After all, a topless woman was a topless woman.

Eagerly, the man pushed her onto his bed, removing the buckle of his pants and sliding them down. Straight to the point, no bother of seduction, as with most of her clients. She slowly slid the skirt of her dress up, her left hand feeling the sheath of her knife and pulling it out.

In one fluid motion, her knife sliced into his leg and he gasped. He barely had the chance to look at the gash and comprehend what was going on before Otra dropped the knife to slide behind him, kicking him behind the knee before kneeing him in his bare crotch. The man buckled as one of her hands gripped his chin. With her other hand, she held the back of his head and twisted to create an audible *crack* before the man's body collapsed to the floor.

My dear, you will die sometime between right now and sixty years from now, her leader's voice echoed in her head.

She wasted no time in redressing herself and searching through his room, moving things around and flipping over furniture to make it look like a robbery. Perhaps it was. She took the money and fine things she could fit on her. *Most in the Phoenix, despite our resilience, will likely be closer to the former, as is the nature of our work.*

Approaching the body, she wiped the blood off her blade with his clothes. She felt no pity for him. Whispers swirled around about the occasional judge's abuse of power. He was definitely one of those who used his position to cover up what he'd do to any girl unlucky enough to be alone with him. She was just sorry she hadn't had the pleasure of meeting him sooner as she wondered how many others he'd forced himself upon. *See, we have mastered the art of patience in a life where time is constantly threatening to run out. How else would we have made it this far?*

Crouching down by the fireplace, she pulled back her sleeve to reveal the Phoenix branding on her forearm, with the standard tallying beside it. *We must carry ourselves as such – in loyalty to that notion, we ensure that to our dying breath, we remember each and every last breath we have watched.*

She held the blade above the fire, letting it tickle the tip of the blade until she felt the metal heat up just enough. Biting her lip, she traced out a forty-fourth tally and blew on the wound to soothe the burning pain to which she had grown accustomed. *We can die in peace knowing our sacrifices were toward a better world, even if our names will be a wisp of a memory, carried away with the breeze.*

As the blade cooled down, she slid it back into the sheath on her upper leg and slid out of the window, looking back one more time before disappearing without a witness or a sound.

SIX

LUMINA

——

Sitting alone at the long table in her tent, Lumina fidgeted with the slice of bread in her hand as the fire crackled. Tearing off small chunks to eat, she rolled her tongue over the crusts and soft center in her mouth as her bare feet idly traced circles in the dirt floor. It was decent bread, especially for a loaf that was packed from a Denordan village one of her operatives had visited two days ago, but she wondered how much better it had tasted fresh.

Sighing at her tiny appetite, she packed the half-slice of bread away in the sack, tying it tightly shut just as Citrina peered in, her hands separating the canvas to open the tent. They both beamed at the sight of each other. Citrina looked like the spitting image of her birth mother, and Lumina always considered it a breath of fresh air whenever the girl returned from scouting.

And especially in such a spirit! Good news must have been awaiting her.

Lumina beckoned her over, and Citrina joined her at the pockmarked table. She was glad to have this moment of privacy with the girl before their scheduled operatives' meeting—especially since she was even earlier than usual. "I take it your scouting went well?"

"You could say that."

Nodding, she gave Citrina permission to go on. "Do tell."

"When in the Padaurean Capital, I met a man."

"A man?" The leader's eyes narrowed a bit, suspicious of what would come next given a slight betrayal in the girl's tone. Citrina was a young woman, and no stranger to men, but the very idea of a possible... involvement—at least past those typically used by the Phoenix—troubled her a bit. Lumina had had more than her fair share of experiences with meeting men, enough to make it near-impossible not to be wary, even with the men she had to trust as scouts and Generals.

"It's not like that! Well, not exactly." A silence followed, and Lumina nodded again, allowing Citrina to continue. "You see, I was just grabbing something to drink at the tavern and ended up conversing with this man. He happened to be the Lieutenant of the Royal Guard in the Capital." She paused before taking her leader's silence as an invitation to go on. "So I did as you taught me and seduced him. After he fell asleep, I scouted the castle itself—"

"How did you get into the castle?"

"He's quite close to the royal family. Apparently, the King himself adopted him as a boy."

"Interesting. Do continue then. What did you find in the castle? No one saw you, did they?"

"Only the guards as he took me inside. But it was dark and my cloak covered my face."

Lumina chuckled in approval. The girl had learned well.

After receiving a nod, Citrina continued. "Anyway, I found an unlocked door, so I snooped and found the office. It was quite messy, but I read letters there, talking about the possibility of arranging the Prince's marriage. Both he and the Lieutenant are in their early twenties, if I had to guess."

"Hmm," Lumina replied pensively. "You'd think they'd *both* be married by now."

"Exactly. But I saw no talk yet of such a union for the Lieutenant, even as the King's adopted son. This could be an opportunity to get inside, to influence the Padaurean kingdom from the top down, if possible. Like Codrin did in Marestra."

Looking at her adopted daughter, the woman felt proud. Citrina had not only ingrained her training and words but also had used it to find opportunities to expand the Phoenix and its influence on a higher and more sophisticated level in the Northwest than ever before. "Yes, you may be right," Lumina said, trying not to give too much away. "And he's not already married?"

The girl shook her head.

"Good. Then I would say, either become his regular bedfellow or his wife. You can write to me about their developments, and we can use that to influence them from the inside out."

Citrina nodded. "This way, it'll probably be easier and leave fewer dead as well."

Lumina glanced down at her own forearm, tallied only twelve times—a shabby comparison to some of her scouts—but she comforted herself in knowing that she had to be the organizer. She looked back up at the girl. "This man, is he handsome?"

Red painted Citrina's cheeks, and she nodded hesitantly, leading the woman to chuckle and continue the questions. "He didn't hurt you, did he?"

The girl shook her head violently. "He was actually… quite gentle, strangely."

"And a high rank at such a young age, he must be quite good…" Lumina mused, staring into the fire and idly playing with the chain on her necklace before shifting her gaze back to her daughter. "I suppose there could be worse prospects and positions for you. You could use him and his resources to continue to refine your own skills as well, if possible. Just don't let anything that might develop distract you from your true mission, my little light."

Citrina scowled. "*Mama*, you know I could never betray you or the Phoenix!"

"And if he inquires about your scars?"

"He hasn't yet, but I can figure it out on the way back. Don't you worry."

Lumina nodded. "Then this is quite the exciting opportunity." She was not one to believe in luck, especially with such dumb luck at that, but even now she couldn't deny how well everything happened to line up.

Just then, Otra popped her head into the canvas opening, her curls bouncing. Narrowing her eyes to see better, Lumina noticed a new, angry red tally on her forearm beginning to scab, and pursed her lips. "Who was it this time?"

Otra grinned. "Someone who, you'd agree, met his fate far too late. Are you ready for the meeting?"

The leader nodded, returning the smile. "Bring everyone in."

By the time the operatives at the base had all settled in, Citrina and Otra were already chatting. Looking around, Lumina also observed the scouts who had come back in time.

Tomila, a black-haired assassin whose dewy face looked innocent enough to draw away from her macabre tendencies, played with a small knife, the blade dancing between her graceful yet callused fingers. Dieri, a newer recruit who had just come back from his first mission scouting in an Eputeri village, fidgeted in his seat. Alut, a more experienced scout who'd just finished a run in Denorda, sat patiently in wait for the next order, his steely, catlike eyes looking at Lumina attentively.

One by one, the scouts described to her the status of their respective places. Dieri and Alut reported an incident where a townsperson was rambling on the street about a conspiracy to put the two nations at war for territorial reasons, since, after all, little border was between them, and neither had seen it necessary to put a fort there.

"This person," Lumina mused, "does he mention us by name?"

Alut nodded gravely. "Sometimes. Seen him myself, ma'am. He's a rambler, treated as a lunatic as everyone still thinks of us as a myth—"

"But nonetheless a potential threat," the leader finished. "He needs to be taken care of, especially since that might interrupt our... aspirations. There's been too much peace on the Continent, and we may need a war at some point if we want to further our mission in any significant way."

The scout nodded. "I can do so as soon as I return."

"No," she responded, "you go there too often. You'd be recognized. We'll send in Tomila to get the job done quickly. She'll be on your tail to get there and then leave as soon as she's finished without compromising your cover."

Tomila looked up. She said nothing, but her stormy gray eyes glittered with anticipation as she nodded.

Alut looked at her hesitantly but nodded as well. "I suppose. As long as she keeps the guy quiet."

The girl gave him a devilish smile. "I'll take him out to the woods so no one hears him."

Dieri shuddered, and Lumina just barely kept in a small chuckle. He had yet to get used to Tomila's... creative tactics, which, by this point, left the others unfazed.

"Now, Otra," Lumina directed, "we have informants in all but one of the Lebirosi cities. You will attend the Festival of the Free in Midstad and take the time to really understand the area. Act as one of them, and use that to find the chinks in their armor. Learn more about the culture and layout of the city and perhaps find an informant or two. Then report back to me at the end of the celebrations."

Otra nodded dutifully, and Lumina turned back to the five scouts who sat ahead of her. "Good chat. You are now dismissed and are to leave at the first light of dawn." Everyone nodded, one by one leaving the tent while the leader made eye contact with Citrina and motioned for her to stay.

After the other scouts filed out, she and Citrina were alone again. She turned back to the girl. "Just be wary. See if you can influence a marriage. You're already twenty, so the age is ripe. And if I recall correctly, the Padaureans value the ties of marriage quite strongly, so they'll have to keep you around, but you have to honor that tie as well if you'd want to fit in with them."

She placed a hand on her daughter's shoulder, smiling warmly as she gently moved a strand of hair out of the girl's face. "As with the others, you should head back tomorrow. I'm glad you came by to tell me. It's good to share our understanding of the situation, face to face, and to let him miss you.

"But return before he forgets about you, and you will be all the more desirable to him when you return. I will let General Herry know that you'll be assigned to Padaure, possibly as a permanent operative, and you will report to him as well as me."

Citrina nodded, returning a grin. "I won't let you down."

SEVEN

LETTA

———

The castle looked like it was the thing of the stories her sister read—pointed, dark gray towers on top of a white castle that was accented with gold and red, on a hilltop surrounded by trees and on the edge of the mountains, separate from the rest of the towns and cities in the kingdom.

As her carriage stopped in front of the castle, two servants immediately walked over to the car to guide her out by one hand each, and another helped bring her bags out and into the castle.

She was greeted by Queen Davena, a regal woman with a petite, slender frame and smooth, inky black hair pulled out of her face in a silky braid. Her porcelain skin shone in the fading golden light of the sunset, and her large gray eyes met Letta's with a kind smile as Col began helping the servants bring the baggage inside.

Her future mother-in-law embraced her warmly, saying, "It is *so* wonderful to meet you, my lovely girl. Since we married off my daughters, being the only lady has been quite lonely."

Letta returned the hug awkwardly, nodding, not sure what to say. She certainly hadn't expected the Queen to greet her alone and couldn't help but wonder where the other members of the royal family were, but she didn't want to be rude. *Be humble,* her father would always say. Perhaps now was the time to put that to the test. She scrambled, trying to recall something from his lectures about easily insulted higher-rank women.

But she didn't have much time for reflection. "Come," the Queen ordered as she pulled away. "Let me show you around. Your father said you might like it here, but I want to make sure for myself that this is a place you can *truly* call home."

She nodded and followed the Queen inside but not before glancing around at one of the gardens outside, decorated with neatly trimmed hedges, patches of flowers, and the occasional sculpture. She locked eyes with a figure in the distance, a tall dark-haired boy who looked not much older than her. He broke eye contact and continued to walk around the garden, musing.

"Forgive Merek," Queen Davena whispered, apparently following the girl's gaze. "He can get moody at times. He just needs a nice walk in the garden. You can meet him later, after he has had his... moment."

Letta gave her a look of confusion, but the woman didn't further acknowledge anything. Something was off, but she couldn't seem to figure out quite what yet. Were they hiding something from her? The Queen's calm composure could almost convince her that nothing was out of the ordinary. Maybe what was normal for these royals was different than what she was used to, yet that strange feeling stuck with her.

She glanced back just as Col gave her a nod and set off, the elegant, dark-brown horses drawing the blue carriage away from the castle, and with it, taking all the familiarity of home as she was left in this new place with beautiful strangers.

Yet those doubts and confusion seemed to wash away upon entering the splendid palace and seeing ornately carved wooden walls and railings joined together with beautifully detailed murals. The Queen took her briefly through the rooms, and Letta observed many fascinating collections ranging from paintings to armories to tapestries. She tried to keep up with the informal tour, noting the many places and names that were rattled off as gift-givers of such beautiful items. She couldn't deny that this palace had a powerful sense of culture, and it was large enough that she felt like she was traveling the Continent herself just by following the Queen from room to room.

Eventually, duty called for Queen Davena, who followed a servant out of the room after giving Letta a quick, polite apology. But the girl didn't mind, although she couldn't say she knew where she was in the castle. There had to be over 150 rooms, much greater than the measly twenty at her home, so she felt like she was on her own little adventure. The place felt foreign to her, but she was sure she'd grow accustomed to it and eventually call it home. However, she couldn't help but revel in the history! The culture! The art! All of that within these walls!

Entering another room, she found that her mother had been right. The library was splendid. Walnut columns with intricately carved bevels and swirls framed shelf upon shelf of multicolored books that filled up at least the first floor of the two-level room, surrounding a small, wooden table with chairs, illuminated by a glass chandelier above. The books neatly filled the shelves, ranging from thick to thin. Some looked older than the kingdom itself while others looked freshly printed. Reading the titles as she gently brushed the book-spines with her fingers, she recognized only a few and was already dying to read the others.

"L-L-Looking for s-something?" Letta dropped her hand to her side and looked to her right to find a skinny, black-haired boy about her height and age. Although, from what she could tell, it wasn't the same boy from the garden. His frame was awkward, with a bit of a hunch and bony arms that he crossed in front of him as he leaned against the column by a small stair entrance in the corner that she hadn't noticed before, and his light gray eyes narrowed.

Realizing she still hadn't responded, she shook her head while sheepishly folding her hands in front of her, as if she'd been caught doing something wrong. By the way this boy was looking at her, maybe she had been.

"This is m-my mother's s-study, you know." He struggled to maintain eye contact, and his stutter was evident, but it didn't seem to stop him from continuing. "I-I-I mean, she always talks a-about how i-important b-books are, b-but, s-s-strangers aren't a-allowed—"

"My boy, that is *no* way to talk to your future sister-in-law now, is it?" a woman said in a calmly assertive manner from above. Both of them looked up to find the Queen standing over them on the second level, her hands dancing on the railing that topped the golden balusters with complex designs of vines above the bookshelves.

The boy flashed Letta a look, one that she didn't have the time to read, before turning back up the stairs and disappearing.

"Please do forgive my son. The boys are definitely… quite interesting," Queen Davena sighed, smiling warmly.

Letta tried to force one in response but said nothing.

The woman continued, her voice smoother than satin. "Kenric is especially protective of these books. He seems to have taken it the most seriously, how I always talk about the importance of education... something that, I have heard, you strongly believe in. Is that right?"

Letta nodded silently, and the woman walked out, coming back through the stairs and joining her at her side. She was a lovely woman with soft features. The girl could most definitely see that her sons were a spitting image of the Queen. Yet, unlike Kenric, the Queen walked with a confident grace as well as a self-assured and commanding authority even though she was slightly shorter than Letta.

"I look forward to having you in the family, lovely Letta. It is *quite* nice that we were lucky enough to find a young lady such as you who understands the importance of the mind. It is a value I have always hoped to be instilled in my grandchildren as well."

"Of course, Your Majesty," the girl responded quietly.

The Queen chuckled. "Rather soon, I will be calling *you* that." She reached out to the bookshelf and grabbed a book. Letta glanced over it to see the title. *The Ancient School of Love and War.* "This is quite an important title. I would highly recommend it if you have not yet read it."

"It's my favorite," the girl blurted out excitedly.

Turning toward Letta, the Queen gave her another warm smile. "You have a copy?"

"Yes! I mean, not with me. I gave it to my sister before I left."

"How kind of you. Giving your copy of a favorite book feels like giving a piece of yourself to someone. I imagine you must love her very much."

"I do," Letta said, blinking to hold back the water she hadn't realized was building up in her eyes. She hadn't thought about it that way, but she couldn't help but realize that's exactly how it felt, and how she already missed her cloud-headed sister.

The Queen placed a soft hand on her shoulder. "Similarly, you are part of this family now. We give only to each other, using that as our strength. This library is yours to peruse whenever you desire. Do you understand?"

Letta blinked again, giving a small nod, embarrassed that she was almost crying in front of a woman she had just met, especially one who was both the Queen *and* her future mother-in-law, the most powerful woman in the Northwest.

"Good," the woman said, placing a soft kiss on Letta's cheek as she slipped the book into her hands. "I am excited. I have *missed* having a daughter."

EIGHT

CITRINA

———

"This seems like a good place to hunt, Odo," an authoritative voice announced, off in the distance. "Tell the rounders to bring the animals here."

"As you wish, sir," another voice replied.

Shit, thought Citrina. It was windy, and she had barely been able to hear these voices in the first place. There was no telling how much time she'd have to hide. Pulling her sack of things around her back, she shimmied up a tree, her heart hammering in her chest as she prayed that whoever it was wouldn't notice her. Of course, there were hunters. From the sound of their polished language, they were at the very least lords, the only ones stupid enough to hunt in *these* woods for the fun of it.

Just as she managed to make it about twenty feet up, mostly hidden from view, the men stepped into her field of vision—a party of about a dozen who had tied their horses to nearby trees, none of their faces familiar. Now she was glad she'd put on her green cloak; she hoped it was enough to camouflage her while she waited for these morons to pass by.

But they didn't. If anything, she could see one of them quite clearly about fifty feet from the base of the tree, by her guess. He wore a fine blue tunic with embroidered gold threads that shone in the rays of sunlight leaking through the leaves of the trees. Under it, dark stockings hugged his legs adorned by fine leather boots, the same color as the brown deerskin with an intricate blackbird design that draped over his shoulders.

Judging by his dress and the fact that the Padaurean Capital had to be less than a league away, she guessed that it had to be the King. It was currently peacetime for Padaure, so it wouldn't be out of the ordinary for the royal man to hunt, to get the thrill of a kill, and feel like a "real man" without having to start a war. To her liking, she didn't notice Jasper in the party. It reassured her to know he wasn't taking part in these frivolous activities.

The King knelt, pulling his crossbow in front of him to aim at something upwind of him. Citrina shifted to see just the antlers of a young stag. She was too far away from it to see much else.

She shifted her gaze back to the group, only to notice a black, beefy figure behind the party, moving silently in their direction. Bringing herself to a lower branch, she realized it was a monstrous boar. It had to be at least four times her mass with shiny gray tusks at least as long as her hand protruding from a crooked snout. The creature's heavy torso moved with its deep breaths. By the way those eyes were trained on the group, Citrina could tell it was hungry. With surprise on the feral creature's side, the party was a meal in waiting.

She glanced at the group ahead. They were so fixated on the stag that they hadn't seemed to notice the boar looming just a few yards behind them, and the wind blowing probably masked the sound of the animal's footsteps. This wasn't going to end well, and the King's potential death would result in chaos upon returning. While political chaos could sometimes be harnessed by the Phoenix, it could also possibly snatch away the opportunity she'd traveled all this way back for. Something had to be done.

Racking her brain, Citrina did her best to recall the lessons she'd gotten from some of the hunters who had joined the Phoenix, trying to remember how she'd killed a boar before. The ones she'd killed in the past had been considerably smaller than this beast, and she'd had a boar spear at the time. Would she be able to handle this armed only with her set of knives?

It was worth a shot. Besides, a boar was a boar, no matter the size. They had thick skulls and thick hides that could stop bolts, so the head and back weren't options... but they still had the same weak spots. As she swung lower and lower, she grabbed one of the larger, sheathed knives concealed by her cloak. The blade was just a little longer than her forearm, and she gripped onto it with her teeth. The animal still hadn't noticed her, to her luck.

As she secured herself, now only ten feet above the ground, she could see it clearly; its sheer size was enough to intimidate anything that would encounter it. But she couldn't turn back now. Brandishing a smaller blade, this one specially made for throwing, she swung under the low branch and jumped down.

The boar didn't even have time to turn around before she landed the smaller knife in the back of its hind knee, severing the tendon and resulting in a piercing squeal that drew attention to it as it stumbled. She was already on the ground, and it was too late to hide from the party, so she disregarded the surprised eyes.

To her dismay, the limp didn't seem to limit the boar much, but its sheer size did make it slow to turn around. And boy, was it not happy. Before she could allow herself to get caught up in her thoughts, she took the opportunity to sprint toward its hind legs and managed to cut the tendon on the back of its functioning hind leg, resulting in another furious cry of pain as it stumbled. Yet it was still dangerous, and she would have to reach underneath for the finishing blow.

Circling around, she slid by its blind spot so her face was just inches away from its massive front hoof, just barely avoiding its attempts to stomp on her. As she plunged the larger blade into the animal's armpit to hear a sickening *squish*, blood splashed onto her face and neck. Closing her eyes momentarily and spitting out the blood, she twisted it deeper in as the creature tried to flail out of her grasp while she held on to its leg tightly. Its angry squeals grew weaker and more desperate as she violently shook the blade from side to side, praying it would end soon.

And it did. The animal let out a large, pained sigh, and she barely managed to roll out of its way as it fell in her direction. She lay on her back, closing her eyes again for a second and gasping for breath, as she let herself rest.

The light that came through her eyelids seemed to dim, and she opened her eyes to find several men standing over her, a mix of apparent shock and concern on their faces. Crouching down, a couple of them reached toward her. She flinched and leaned against the bulky carcass, bringing her legs to her torso and pulling away as she sat up.

"Don't touch me," she growled.

"The woman just took down a monster of a boar. I would suggest we listen to her," said that clear, authoritative voice, and she looked up to find the man in blue walking toward her. His men nodded and stepped away from her, clearing a path for him.

"Greetings, miss. I am King Miran of Padaure. It is a pleasure to make your acquaintance." He bowed politely. Citrina found it quite strange that a royal was bowing to *her*, a strange woman covered in mud and boar's blood, but she remembered that Padaureans placed a large emphasis on politeness. "What might be your name, young woman?"

She hesitated, glancing at the faces of the men who continued to stare at her before looking back at him and swallowing, trying not to gag at the metallic taste from the blood still in her mouth. "Onyx."

"Well, Onyx, perhaps you would like to join us? We will get you cleaned up, and I would be charmed to hear the interesting story I imagine you have that led you to fight better than half my men."

Citrina said nothing. He stretched out a hand, offering a kind half-smile that reached his lavender eyes as well. "Please, I ask of you, allow me to at least repay you for saving our lives."

Gingerly, she decided to take his hand as he helped her to her feet, trying not to pay attention to the eyes of all the men around them. The King looked around and chuckled. "Eyes off, men, do not act like you have never seen a woman before. Perhaps you can make yourselves useful and pack this beast up? We will have a nice feast upon our return." The men looked down quickly and shamefully, nodding in choruses of, "Yes, Your Majesty."

The King turned around, inviting her with a hand to join him at his side. "So what brings you to the Padaurean forests?"

Citrina took a breath, remembering the alias she'd had the last time she'd been in the kingdom, on her scouting mission, and she wondered if she could modify and summarize it in time. "Your Majesty, I work as a huntress. Been traveling on my own for a while to find work, and the main roads aren't the best place for a woman."

"So you take the forest, filled with beasts."

"Your Majesty, the main road is filled with beasts of its own."

On the way back, sitting on a horse that one of the men had politely insisted she mount, Citrina found that the King loved to talk and ask questions as he rode by her side. She did her best to respond, making up answers on the spot that she hoped were convincing enough whenever they got too personal.

He questioned everything: her hometown, which she said was a Northern Inecori village; how long she'd been hunting—as long as she could walk; how she learned to speak so well—travel and experience working with clients and locals of varying ranks. To her credit, she didn't have to lie very much so long as she remained vague.

Finally, he asked her about her parents and she went silent. Luckily, he seemed to take the hint and changed the subject to ask her other questions.

When they finally got to the castle, just as magnificent as she'd remembered it, he instructed servants to take her to the baths and get her cleaned and changed. After the ladies had wiped off all the blood and dirt from her skin and placed her in a form-fitting, light pink gown, another servant walked into the room. "The King has requested your presence at the table, my lady."

Citrina nodded and followed him to the hall to find the King by himself, still in his hunting regalia. The servant pulled out a seat that she politely took, thanking him as he disappeared into the royal kitchen to leave her alone with the monarch.

"Dinner is not for another hour, but I wanted to speak with you, alone this time," the King said.

She swallowed nervously and nodded.

He continued, "Forgive me for inquiring so much. You strike me as a fascinating one. I have yet to see many of the beasts in my own army become half as competent as you, and so well-trained at that, even forgetting the fact that you *are*... well... a lady.

"At least the things in the forest pose a challenge or put up a fight. Would you not agree?"

Citrina nodded again, and he went on. "I need more like you in my army. I have been stuck recruiting farmers' boys who can barely wield a sword when sober... and often some of them are not, no thanks to my own son's influence. Perhaps your presence would motivate the others to do better."

"I am honored, my King, but I fear you esteem me too highly."

He laughed heartily, a jolly sound that filled the room with its warm timbre. "You remind me of my best. He is also far too humble. The two of you might get along."

"Is that so?" She swallowed, wondering if she knew who he was talking about. Either way, this opportunity, at the King's word no less, seemed too great to turn down. It was better than the likes of what she'd come for, even if he didn't realize it.

"I will introduce you to him, should you decide to accept my offer."

"Forgive my asking, but what might that entail?"

"Like the rest, you will have your own chambers in the soldiers' quarters and be fed, clothed, and treated well, if not better than them. You will train with the other soldiers, and *if* you prove yourself to them as well—which, from what I have seen, is quite likely—you may go up the ranks with your own men to lead, should we enter any... conflict."

"Your Majesty, do you think war to be likely? With whom?"

He shrugged, looking into her eyes sternly. "We have political arrangements with other kingdoms to avoid war, but it helps to keep a sense of authority within our own land in case any lord gets too... confident." Pausing for a second, he momentarily broke eye contact to look at the floor before shaking his head and continuing as if his thoughts hadn't trailed off at all. "Anyway, there would be a new rule, as you are the first woman here, which invariably can lead to complications if not addressed immediately."

"What might that be?"

"No... *involvement*... with the other soldiers, preferably with anyone." He paused, looking at her as if to read her reaction. "This is just to avoid complications and conflicts of interest. Of course, with the fact that there have been only men so far, we didn't have to worry about that until now.

"Should you decide you want someone, outside of the soldiers, of course, and want to commit to a family instead, I will grant you dismissal if you are to be married. This is no life for a mother, nor for a wife.

"Should you choose a fellow soldier, that would be considered a... conflict of loyalty."

"You mean treason," she asked. The King nodded. "Which I assume is punishable by death."

The King hesitantly nodded again. "We cannot afford to have any internal complications within the Guard."

Citrina took a deep breath. She could no longer hold out hope of being a wife or a bedfellow to the Lieutenant if she agreed to the terms, but it would be a small price to pay for the influence she could have and the power she could wield on behalf of the Phoenix. Besides, it was bound to be more interesting and fun than her original intent. She'd been taught to court and seduce, and she didn't mind doing it when necessary, but the idea of having her own soldiers to lead, and with the King's permission, no less! She could direct her men to do whatever she pleased, whether on her terms or those of the Phoenix, without even having to suggest opening her legs.

She glanced back at the door to the kitchen where she could smell that the boar was being prepared for the royals to have their dinner. It had been a magnificent beast, a killing machine with tusks like silver perfect for mowing down anything in its way. Originally, she had felt a bit sorry for killing it. But it placed a greater opportunity in her hands, and for that she silently thanked it.

Meeting the eyes of the King, she nodded, revealing a small smile. "I would be honored to accept, Your Majesty."

NINE

JASPER

With his arms crossed, Jasper watched two men wrapped around each other and rolling on the ground of the soldiers' courtyard, a half-acre of patches of grass and dust and dirt surrounded by the stone perimeter of the barracks. The wiry one on the bottom had locked his arms around the larger one's neck and his legs around the man's waist as dust clouds billowed around the two.

"Good work. Call it," Jasper fibbed, a bit exasperated at the poor form but too tired to correct them yet another time for today. But he couldn't leave them off without any feedback. "Though, Alard, it shouldn't be so easy for your opponent to get you in that position, especially so quickly and with someone as scrawny as Osbert."

"Hey!" exclaimed Osbert, warranting a half-apologetic shrug from his Lieutenant.

"I'll keep a weapon on me body to avoid 'at," Alard replied as he rolled onto his hands and knees, propping himself up to face Jasper with a cough as he inhaled some of the dust.

"Even weapons are useless in that position, my good man." Jasper slapped a friendly hand on Alard's shoulder. "Ask your friend over there for advice, and in return, you can offer him work on his swordsmanship." The soldier nodded and walked over to join the small group with Osbert as they headed toward their quarters.

"Jasper," the King called. He turned to find King Miran standing there, in his typical blue tunic and cloak of deerskin.

"Back from the hunt, I see, sir." Jasper smiled at him, walking over to meet his adoptive father and receiving a smile back as they strolled around the perimeter of the emptying courtyard. The men filed into the barracks, housed in the three stories of stone that surrounded them.

"Oh, and what a hunt it was! I tell you, you *must* join me on these things, you miss a lot," Miran exclaimed, his face red with excitement.

"I prefer to focus on targets that involve my duty to protect Your Majesty."

"Yes, yes, I am sure," the King waved a dismissive hand, "but even in my forty-three years, I can *still* say there are new things out there to be seen, especially with this hunt!"

"I would love to hear of it at dinner," Jasper said politely, starting to turn back before the King grasped his arm.

"Actually, this concerns you as well, something I think is better said sooner than later. It is why I wanted to talk to you before dinner." The Lieutenant raised an eyebrow curiously, and Miran continued. "There was a monstrous boar, the likes of which I have not seen in years, if at all. I wish I could have said I saw it creep behind us, but our focus was on this *magnificent* stag ahead of me."

Jasper's eyes widened as his brows narrowed incredulously. "It attacked the group?"

"Thank the heavens, no! That is what was so remarkable. It died before it had the chance to get too close."

"What killed it?"

"Not what. Who. A woman."

Jasper snorted, rolling his eyes. "So you'll tell me that despite a group of... what? A dozen men? The largest hog you've ever seen was killed by some *woman*? With all due respect, Your Majesty, you should be saving your jokes for the dinner table."

But the King's face was serious, and Jasper's smile dropped as they stopped by the tall iron gates that led to the main entrance of the soldiers' yard. The Lieutenant turned to look at him.

"You should have seen it, Jasper," the King said softly, stiffness in his tone. "It took her less than a minute to do it. She moved as if it were instinctual. I have never seen anything killed so smoothly."

The Lieutenant swallowed. "So, where did she go... you know... after that? Did she disappear?"

"I invited her for a chat, and she seemed very well-spoken. Apparently, she had a rough life—an orphan on the streets, poor thing—but became a huntress and traveled enough to pick up some useful skills. She is a sharp one, she is."

"Must be, if she's survived this long in that forest, presumably on her own."

"Yes, yes, very much so. And she has been looking for work and a place to stay. So I offered her one. In the soldiers' chambers."

Jasper was appalled at the notion and even a bit frightened for the King. "You dishonor a woman, one you claim to be better at killing than most of our men, by offering her a place in their beds?" He nervously ran a callused hand through his hair. If she really was as good as Miran was talking her up to be, even the Guard might not stand in her way if she were to take offense.

After looking at Jasper with a momentary perplexed expression, he let out a chuckle, patting a hand on Jasper's arm. "Of course not, my good son. I offered her a position of joining the Guard. After all, we can never be too prepared for any instance."

The Lieutenant nodded, still a bit uneasy. "Agreed, but she is a stranger. Is she not?"

"As are the other recruits. But at least she is a competent one."

He sighed, frustrated that the King hadn't mentioned anything to him before making the offer. But he was King, and Jasper was too tired to argue with him. "What did she say?"

"She accepted, to my gratitude. So I would like you to keep an eye on her and update me concerning how she progresses and whether she's any trouble. I think you would like her; the two of you seem similar."

"How so?"

"Quick and quiet, to the point, looking for the most effective ways of doing things. And I daresay she might be even able to rival you."

"Hm." If all this was true, and Miran wasn't just exaggerating, perhaps he'd feel less drained at practices. Maybe it'd even present a good example and a new sense of competition to his men.

"There *is* another thing that needs to be addressed here," Miran continued. Jasper nodded again, cueing him to continue, and the King leaned in close. "She is quite a pretty one. I know your integrity exceeds any temptation you might have, but I am unsure if we can say the same for the recruits… Perhaps talk to them and let them know not to try anything. I have made her abstinence a condition of the opportunity, and she agreed. You know what treason would result in, and she does as well."

"Forgive my asking, sir, but wouldn't that be a bit extreme to call that treason, especially regarding the... activities... of the other men in their free hours?"

"Perhaps, but it is a necessary caution. Women run a higher risk of consequences for their actions than do men."

Jasper pretended to agree, figuring it would be in poor taste to bring up that it might be prejudice encouraged by the late Queen's fate.

"And we both know that training grounds are barely the place for the typical woman, surely not for a mother, wife, or child."

"I suppose." The Lieutenant looked around at the empty courtyard, his eyes flitting around and looking past the gate to the street, already finding some of his men in pursuit of drinks and women while others shuffled to their watch posts at various spots in the castle. He turned back to the King. "Where is she now?"

"I believe she is currently in her new bedchamber. If you would like, we can go over and I can introduce the two of you."

"That sounds like a fine idea," Jasper said then gestured toward the stone building ahead of them, inviting the King to lead the way.

Miran nodded, taking the lead across the dusty courtyard and brushing off his cloak in the late afternoon's rays as they reached and swung open the wooden door. They proceeded into the darker hallways, continuing until they reached a door to a room that he'd previously known to be empty.

The King knocked firmly on the door three times. "Pardon, my lady, I would like to briefly introduce you to the Lieutenant."

A silence ensued for a couple of seconds before a familiar voice replied, "Come in."

Beaming proudly at Jasper, Miran slowly opened the door to find long fingers brushing a strand of long, dark honey-colored hair out of the woman's face as she stood up. It appeared she had just finished setting up the knives on her bedside table. But this wasn't just any woman. He recognized her even before they locked eyes.

TEN

OTRA

The square was beautifully lit despite the darkness that fell over the city, with lanterns flooding every inch of space that wasn't taken up by people. Otra had never seen such a crowd, much less such a happy one. Children chased each other with purple paint on their faces while their parents laughed and danced, happy to have the excuse to be out and feel young again. She watched the youths who blushed when dancing with each other and listened to the music and singing that seemed to be coming from all directions.

The Festival of the Free was the biggest celebration in the Allied Cities of Lebiros—taking place every mid-spring to celebrate the unification of the five regions—and the locals took it incredibly seriously. Even the city officials were out, barely distinguishable from the common people themselves in this setting, although their clothing still looked more expensive than the others', naturally.

From what she had seen, Midstad was a large city, filled with cobblestone streets and bustling commoners. Some of the tallest buildings reached as high as four or five stories. She'd wandered through the entirety today but had lost her way a couple of times, which told her that Lumina was right to give her the month to gather information on the city. The streets were complex, and many of the buildings looked the same. Their height was the only way she could estimate where she was, as the tallest ones dominated the center of the town.

Otra kept to herself, leaning against one of the open-air countertops that had been set up to serve drinks for the people. As complex as the city was, she was honored to be able to scout here for Lumina's case. This was the last city they needed informants for, and she could see why they relied on them in Lebiros. Who better to understand the complexities of the city than a local? Especially when a stranger like her would need at least a year to have an idea of even half of what was constantly happening in the biggest cities in the South.

Taking advantage of the festivities, her eyes scanned the scene to note and memorize the faces of each of the officials she could identify, hoping to learn their names at some point, preferably from a distance. She had the luck of attending this spectacle for informational purposes. As long as she gave Lumina all the information she could find on Lebirosi happenings and remained invisible among these people, she could do as she pleased here. That was just the way she liked it, and the spirit of the atmosphere only filled her lungs up with that sense of freedom.

Closing her eyes, she breathed in the scent of sweet wines and honey that floated through the air and then opened them again to continue exploring the crowd. As her gaze shifted, she found herself locking eyes with those of a beautiful stranger, a tall man with dark, curly hair and even darker eyes. The clothing that hugged his body was too fine to be of commonfolk, yet he didn't dress as lavishly as the councilmembers either. He must have been working as a council advisor.

She couldn't bring herself to look away from his eyes, especially with the intense spark that seemed to light them up.

He might have potential, her conscience told her as she shook her head, realizing she was smiling at him and biting her lip, out of habit from seducing men like him. As he began to approach her, she broke off eye contact and blanked her expression. *But first, focus on what Lumina sent you to do. He'll be around later.*

Listening to that voice, she slipped from her spot and wove through the crowd, looking back only when she had made it to the other side and snuck into an alley, ensuring she'd lost him.

The second night, she wasn't so lucky. She had tried to avoid the crowd this time, walking on a parallel street with fewer people, though comparing to that crowd wasn't saying much.

Her throat burned from the thirst she'd worked up by being on her feet the past few days. Again, she'd spent the day walking through the streets multiple times, dedicating its entirety to note different and better ways to get in, out, and around. It would make her work, and that of the Phoenix, much easier, especially with the maps she could draw from memory. Often she would create them upon her return from a scouting, as making any while on her missions could create suspicion and jeopardize her operations if somehow found.

But she decided to take that risk this time. The city was too large to rely on memory alone, so she relied on keeping small pieces of maps stashed in her bag, which she'd left at the inn in this part of town.

Sitting down in one of the few available seats, she ordered a water and swallowed the entire cupful in one go. As she placed it down, she found someone sliding a seat by her side and slipping into it. The man from the day before.

He definitely recognized her as well, and his eyes absolutely refused to leave hers as they seemed to survey her with a confident curiosity. As the barman walked past, he wasted no time in ordering drinks for the both of them.

Otra broke the eye contact to say, "None for me, please." She batted her eyelashes delicately with a sweet smile, and the flustered barman nodded and only gave a drink to the man by her side.

The stranger smirked. "Not an easy one, are you?"

She leaned back in her chair and crossed her legs, drumming her fingertips on the tabletop as she looked back at him while he took a sip of his brandy. With a half-smirk, she replied, "Depends who's asking, and it doesn't seem to be the case for you."

He placed a hand on his heart with a superficial look of offense. "Ouch," he replied with a chuckle, placing his cup down and leaning in closer to offer his hand. "At least one dance? The music here is rather nice, and it *is* tradition. It would be a crime not to."

Raising an eyebrow, Otra replied, "Is it really?"

"As a man with a legal trade, I can say it is not," he chuckled, "unfortunately. But still quite nice."

She hesitated. He worked in law, making him a risky person to talk to, especially now that he could recognize her. Yet perhaps he would be a valuable source as well, and it didn't hurt that he was quite attractive, much more so than the men she usually seduced. Nodding, she gently slipped her hand into his. After all, what harm could one dance do?

He squeezed her hand and gave her a warm smile, pulling her to the dance area in the midst of the crowd and starting to lead. Otra was impressed. Never had she danced with someone who knew the steps so well, much less with such grace as he did, both of them light on their feet and matching one another in rhythm.

Her stomach fluttered as he spun her, and at the end of the spin, he pulled her closer, their faces inches away from each other with her back against his chest. His muscular arm crossed her torso as his hand held hers, while the band played the final notes of the song. They froze in that position, and Otra's mouth was left slightly agape, her thoughts jumbled. She looked into those eyes that reflected the lanterns that surrounded them, and his skin took on a dark golden tone in the lights.

"Would it be possible for me to learn the name of such a beautiful dancer?" he whispered in her ear, his breath tickling her neck and sending shivers up her spine as the next song began.

Blinking, she came back to her senses and rolled her eyes, now sure about his aims. Men always used flattery to try to get closer, but she wanted to focus on collecting information, not on entertaining people like him. Even if she allowed herself to get too involved, it would only make it harder for her to flee after finishing her work. She began to try and pull away, but his arm didn't budge as she looked back up, her eyes tracing his fine jawline up to his eyes.

"The name is Vitor," he told her, obviously trying to solicit hers.

She stopped moving and looked back at him. "Daniela," she said, using one of her aliases.

He chuckled and loosened his grip on her as she gingerly slipped out. "Perhaps you're a clever liar to an honest man, but I cannot pretend it works on me," he called to her, and she turned to look at him incredulously as he stood there, watching her every movement as if he were taking her in. Looking him up and down, she paused for a moment as the heat rose to her cheeks before she fled from him for the second night in a row.

ELEVEN

———

The young maiden wandered behind the mill as Petyr had said. Sure enough, there he was, pacing back and forth in anticipation as the golden rays reached out over the fields and enveloped them both. When he saw her, he seemed to freeze for a moment. His eyes traced her outline before he shook his head and walked over to her.

"Turn around," he instructed. Apprehensively, she obliged. "Now close your eyes."

"What're you doing?"

"Just trust me on this. Have I ever done you wrong?"

"No, but only because you weren't caught yet." She smirked.

He scoffed in mock horror. "You wound me."

She giggled as she felt his hands brush her hair to the side, and something cool traced the top of her breast. Her eyes opened, and she peered down to find a fine gold chain around her neck with a lovely emerald the size of a small coin at one end of the loop. With a gasp, she whirled around to face him. "Where did you get this?"

He shrugged but failed to hide his mischievous grin. "It was lying around."

"How did you manage to pull this off? Why would you do this? Do you realize...?" She trailed off when his hand cupped her face, ever so gently, and her breath caught in her throat. Her hand slowly traced from his other elbow down his skinny forearm, and he winced as she accidentally brushed the wounds on it. She flinched and gasped quietly, sorry for forgetting about them. They were a gift from his father—one of the reasons she knew Petyr liked to stay out as much as he could.

He sat down and leaned against the mill, staring out over the fields the hilltop oversaw and the clouds that blotted the now-orange horizon. She joined him, shuffling and leaving just a bit of space between them, enough to be close to him but not too close, so she could pretend to be as nonchalant as he seemed.

Petyr sighed, and a short silence followed that she wasn't sure how to break. When she looked over, all thoughts of having to appear composed disappeared as she observed his own fidgeting. She was relieved when he decided to start speaking again. "One day, I'll escape from this wretched town. I'll rise to the top. Build a better life for those beneath. I'll do whatever it takes to make the best life for them and the family I'll have."

He turned to her, the powerful sunlight illuminating his beautiful golden skin and those rich eyes. "I realize I'm still poor. I'm still a thief. But I swear I-I'll do it. And there's only one person I can even imagine bringing along." He took her hands in his, grasping them with a pleading glimmer in his eyes. "Run away with me."

She wasn't quite sure what to say. She just stared at him incredulously, her mouth opening to say something but closing again when the words didn't come to her.

Noting her silence, Petyr continued. "We... we don't have to do it right away. I'm willing to wait as long as it takes." His

gaze dropped to her hands and he gave them a short squeeze.
"I want to make a beautiful life for you, one that's better than
the hell we've had to grow up in.

"I just hoped a necklace could work until I find the money
to buy you a proper ring... But if you don't like it o-or don't
want anything to do with this or me, maybe I can—"

She interrupted him with an impulsive but light kiss, his
lips even softer than she'd imagined.

As she pulled away, he smiled and shifted her onto his lap,
wrapping his arms around her waist and kissing her on the
shoulder. She traced his cheekbone with her thumb and ran
her hand through his light brown locks.

"Let's leave in a week's time," she decided, and her heart
filled up from the joy she saw in his eyes.

TWELVE

LETTA

___

With the afternoon sun dancing just above the treetops and seeping in through the sparse clouds and rectangular windows, Letta finished settling into the temporary quarters she would inhabit before the wedding.

The place was quiet. With the exception of the servants and the strange interaction with the Queen and younger Prince, the Princess-to-be had spent the time alone. The King and Queen were probably busy with political matters, while the Princes were off doing… What was it they did in their spare time?

This castle was the largest she'd ever seen, and she hadn't even seen all of it. Other people *had* to be around, but she had so much time to herself, left to her own devices for the most part. Not that she minded. She enjoyed time alone and wondered how she could spend it. She hadn't been here for more than a day, and she had yet to explore it in depth: the halls, the art, the garden—the garden! That was the place to go, and one of the things she had missed the most about home.

Slipping out, she wandered the premises, trailing along the stone walkways, perfectly arranged in square tiles, and observing the neatly trimmed hedges, with fountains and statues of Apasian Kings peppering the area. Her hand traced along the beveled yet sleek stone banister as she overlooked the downhill meadow that was surrounded by tall evergreen trees.

"Quite nice, is it not?" came a silvery voice by her right side.

Letta flinched, startled to find a slightly familiar boy standing little more than a foot away and leaning over the same banisters as he took in the view. When he turned to her, the eyes she met were so blue it seemed as though they had stolen the color from the sky. By the time she realized she was staring and found it in her to give a nod, she could feel her cheeks warm up as she curtsied.

"Apologies, my lady," he said, glancing down as he gave a slight bow before looking back at her and taking her hand in his. "I have been told that I am quiet, but startling you was not my intention." His lips brushed the top of her hand.

Her heart hammered in her chest. She wasn't sure how she'd imagined her future husband to look like, but she couldn't complain. Now she could see why her sister could so easily fall into an obsession with stories about Princes and Princesses. It was at once a beautiful and odd feeling to experience it in reality, her stomach fluttering now that she realized perhaps those stories weren't completely false. But she was a realist. This man couldn't be *that* perfect. Something had to be wrong with him. Perhaps he was dumb.

Another too-long silence followed before she nodded again, slipping her hand out of his to smooth her dress and look back at the view. "I've been told the same."

He chuckled. "I have heard that's not the only thing we have in common—from what I have heard about our parents' discussions, at least."

"Oh?" Her head turned back to Prince Merek as she arched an eyebrow, trying to pretend that her mother hadn't said the same. "What might you have heard? "

"Something about spending too much time with gardens and books," he replied, a tiny smirk creeping in, and she couldn't help but return it.

"Is that so?" She raised an eyebrow apprehensively.

"Unless I have been deceived."

"Even if so, two people may both enjoy books and gardens yet differ entirely in every other fashion," she chaffed, turning her body to face him.

"Those differences are all the more to learn from. I consistently find myself fascinated by the intricate stories people unknowingly tell through their actions."

"Or it could lead to quarrels, which make for more harm than good."

He chuckled a little, revealing pearl-white teeth, and he looked out over the treetops. "Then let it be of the thoughtful sort, of which we are wary—the fastest way to turn the thoughtful into thoughtless is through rebuking criticism or even the shadow of its threat."

Hmm, perhaps he has potential. "One could say the same for the reverse," Letta challenged, the fingers on her left hand drumming on the top of the banister.

He looked back at her, and with a tiny step, he was incredibly close to her. She was close enough to see the outer dark gray ring of his eyes and the light that reflected in his dark eyelashes when he looked down. "I imagine we'll have the time to learn which is our circumstance." Their faces were just inches away from one another as his hand grazed down the back of her arm to lightly take her hand into his.

"I suppose we will," she whispered quietly, their eyes meeting for a moment that immobilized her as he brought her hand up to kiss it again.

A throat-clear startled them, and her hand slipped out of his as she stepped back to smooth her dress. She hoped her cheeks weren't too red as she looked up to see the spindly figure of her Prince's brother, who stood there staring at them.

"My apologies," Kenric said, his apology flat and toneless, before continuing, "b-but it's time f-f-for dinner, b-before it gets too d-d-dark."

Her eyes went back to those of Merek, who was looking at his brother with a nod. "You're right," he replied and offered his arm to Letta. "We tend to eat a bit earlier than most, usually before the sun sets."

"Why is that?" she asked, tilting her head curiously as she took it.

He sighed, looking back to Kenric and sharing a look with his brother that she couldn't read. "Call it a family tradition."

The dining room looked quite like the other rooms she had seen thus far in the palace. The walls were lined and beveled by a rich brown walnut, the fireplace and entryways meticulously carved with designs similar to those of the library. The carpets were of a splendid, multicolored pattern as well that lined up perfectly with the layout of the room. Here, even the chairs were incredibly cushioned and intricately designed, arranged neatly around a green-clothed table, with tiny designs of deer—the Apasian heraldic animal—stitched into the hems.

As soon as she was seated, a golden-edged plate with some sort of fish was placed in front of her. It was freshly cooked from the smell of it, and she took in its pleasant scent, wondering what sort of cooking was done to make it smell unimaginably better than the river fish she'd smelled before back home.

Only now did she realize how hungry she was, but she still looked around and waited for the cue to start. After all, she couldn't forget her manners, and it wouldn't make a good impression on this new family-to-be if she were the first to start.

"Ever had cod?" King Dobrilo, seated at the head of the table, inquired. He was a dark brown-haired man not much younger than her own father. Queen Davena took a seat at the other head of the table.

"I must say, I don't believe I have, Your Majesty," Letta confessed.

"Well, now that everyone is here, I do invite you to try a bite!" the Queen insisted, beaming. For a moment, Letta was struck by how similar her lovely, enigmatic smile was to Merek's.

The girl nodded in response, looking over to her Prince, who shared a shy glance with her but remained silent.

"And we will raise a toast to the strengthening of our countries' alliance that is to come in the near future," Davena confidently announced, shortly followed by servants shuffling in and pouring wine.

Wine? Letta had never tried anything of the sort before, and the Queen seemed to notice her hesitation. "Are you quite alright, my child?"

The girl nodded again, a little bit more vigorously now. "I... I must admit, I have not quite tried wine, Your Majesty," she revealed. "My father seemed to think it was unfit for a girl." Her eyes widened and she shut her mouth, worrying that she may have inadvertently insulted her future mother-in-law.

The Queen chuckled, and with a wave of the hand assuaged Letta's worries. "Nonsense. Wine is never unfit for a *lady* if she takes care not to indulge in too much of it. Please, do try. I insist."

Letta looked around at the Princes seated across from her, noticing that Kenric's eyes had awkwardly darted from her to his food as he picked at it with his fork. Merek and the King seemed similar, quiet in the face of the Queen, but they'd started to cut into their food. So the girl took that as her cue to begin as well, taking a sip of wine and trying not to make a face at the bitter taste.

"I must reiterate," the Queen started again, "it is nice to have an additional member at the table. It has been quiet since we married off the girls."

"Oh?" Letta arched an eyebrow curiously, a small chunk of fish suspended in the air by the fork in her hand. "Sisters?"

The woman nodded. "Two of them. One of them married into the Denordan royal family, the other to one of the Cer-curan Princes." Her smile turned nostalgic. "In fact, I see a lot of them in you."

"You flatter me, Your Majesty." Letta blushed, twirling the fork in her hand.

"Not so. But I would like, if you are interested, to hand you some of the books they had left behind."

The girl's head snapped back up, meeting the glinted eyes of the Queen. Allowing her into the library so soon was one thing, but gifting her the very books that belonged to her future sisters-in-law? "I—"

"You would like that. Would you not?"

"I would!" Letta exclaimed and then realized she might be too excited for a lady at the dinner table. "If it is at your convenience, Your Majesty."

"Please, Lady Letta. You are soon to become 'Your Majesty' yourself. No need for that formality. You may call me Davena," she responded, "and I will have the servants bring some over to your chambers to read after our meal."

"If you insist," the girl responded hesitantly, watching the expectant eyes of the Queen, "Davena."

The woman nodded. "Lovely," she said, letting silence fall over the table that the men at the table seemed to welcome and that Letta could not break. She couldn't wait to get better acquainted with her family, nor could she help herself in daydreaming about the wonderful conversations and moments to come.

THIRTEEN

JASPER

———

The recruits and current soldiers alike stood in an organized fashion in the dawn light that had just started to illuminate the soldiers' courtyard. Jasper tried not to look at his newest recruit, with her dark pants and a soft gray shirt that covered her enough to not reveal too much skin but not enough to hide her form.

Luckily, it seemed that even though it was obvious the other recruits noticed her, they heeded their Lieutenant's order and treated her normally, albeit with more distance than their other comrades, out of caution. Neither Jasper nor Onyx had mentioned their previous experience with the other, and he didn't see a reason to. What would the King say? And if she was truly as valuable as Miran thought she could be, it would be quite a waste for the Lieutenant not to at least see for himself whether she could be of any use.

He nodded in approval at the short time it had taken the new recruits to prepare themselves, already knowing to separate themselves from the slightly more-experienced men. Even if they weren't yet proficient to the level he wanted, he appreciated that at least they put in effort for their discipline.

"Today will be a mix of drills," he announced as he walked in front of them, about thirty men in all. He looked at the first group of more experienced men. "You veterans will go over to the north side there and practice your grappling." He glanced at the smaller second group of just under a dozen new recruits from the other week. "You will practice blade throws."

A sea of nods ensued as the groups split, and he led the latter to a grassless clearing where a series of pine boards were set up beside each other. Dragging his feet through the dust, he drew two lines parallel to the targets' surfaces, one at about a ten-foot distance, the other at fifteen. Picking up a couple of smaller silver blades by their leather hilts, he walked in front of the group that stood at attention, eyeing his every step.

"Most, if not all, of you may be new to this. Don't fret. It's a lot simpler than you may think and quite useful. As far as I know, we are the only Guard on this side of the Continent that trains their men with blade throws in recent times, so it puts us at an advantage should a conflict break out."

Holding one blade up in his hand, he explained to them the grip and how to hold the knife. He finished the demonstration with the fluid motion that had become a habit of his. Bending his arm squarely as he reached over his head and turned to fling it at the target, he felt that bit of satisfaction from the *thunk* as it sank into the center of the target.

Turning back to the recruits, he finished up his instruction. "Throw from the closer line until you get ten hits in the larger circle, and then move back and go for another ten hits. It's harder than it looks until you figure out what technique works best for you.

"Let me know if you need any help, and please, for your fellow soldiers' sakes, do try to aim for the board and *only* the board."

A few chuckles broke out from the recruits as they moved to begin their drills.

Walking over to the other group, he critiqued their form but was surprised to see it was less necessary. It seemed Alard had taken his advice. He had Osbert pinned to the ground, the clouds of dust billowing around them and the imprints that Osbert left as he smacked the ground to prompt a release from his partner. Perhaps his words weren't falling on deaf ears after all, and maybe he could rest a little knowing his tiny force was improving in their potential to bring pride to the kingdom.

With a small hopeful smile on his face, he turned to the recruits with a refreshed sense of hope for them as well, only for it to disappear as he was met with stark silence rather than the *thuds* and *clangs* he was supposed to be hearing. Picking up his pace as he walked over, he followed the gaze of the men who weren't doing much but staring with their mouths agape at the only woman.

If she noticed the silence and stares, she gave no hint of it as she strolled toward her target. While she pulled the knives she had perfectly landed in the tiny middle circle, Jasper noticed a few small chips of wood that had darted into the ground, not to mention footprints a few feet behind the lines he had drawn as well. It seemed that someone had decided to challenge herself.

"Is there any issue, sir?" asked a silvery voice, and he looked up to meet those stern, dark gray eyes made into a vibrant almost-blue in the sunlight that hit them. Onyx's arms were crossed behind her back, her posture straight in attention and her hair pulled back into a braided bun with a few loose hairs.

After briefly glancing at the target and noting the fact that the only new marks in it were concentrated in the middle, far surpassing the others' hits, he met her gaze again, aware that all eyes were on the two of them.

"Not at all," he said in his best effort to be nonchalant. "Actually, you seem to be doing splendid work. Perhaps you're getting bored?"

"Whether or not I am bored is irrelevant, Lieutenant, as long as I'm following orders and improving," she replied with a polite nod, and her expression was so serious he almost couldn't believe it was the same sultry woman he had seen just a few weeks before. He almost wondered if that night had all been a dream.

A corner of Jasper's mouth turned up, approving of her response. "I see the King was right about you."

She nodded again, glancing down at her feet modestly before looking back up at him with pink cheeks.

"While I am one to believe in rote practice, I doubt these blade drills will help improve your skills any further. Go over and join the other group for now. We'll see how you do in grappling."

"Thank you, sir. I'll do my best," Onyx responded and floated over to join them.

Turning around, he flashed the seasoned men a warning look to remind them to be careful with her, only looking away after he saw their nods.

Jasper pivoted to the recruits, who seemed to just now come to their senses. "Come on now, men. If you were half as proficient, I'd be offering the same." Another chorus of,

"Yes, sirs," and *clangs* ensued with the occasional *thud* of a successful landing.

The Lieutenant had a hard time tearing his eyes away from the way her limber body twisted and caused every man she was up against in grappling to submit. She was somewhat tall, but by no means the largest of them, but her agile responses and manipulations of leverage seemed near-reflexive to her, especially compared to the men who, admittedly, needed the practice. Sergeant Tarren stood by Jasper as they watched her take down another soldier—Tarren's younger brother Alard, a burly man slightly taller than her—in her chokehold.

"Some of us are bettin' she could take you," Tarren whispered with a chuckle.

"I see what you're doing, and it's not going to work," Jasper breathed emotionlessly, not taking his sight off the figure on top of the man who was slamming his hand on the ground.

"Not sayin' an'thin', sir," Tarren replied, and a grin grew on his face. "But she's beaten all our asses. What's she gonna do now, go through a second round of us? As if we had the time to recover."

"Just th' one time, *please*," Osbert joined in, along with a couple of his men who had seemed to overhear. "Jus' a girl, nothin' to be scared of, and it'll be somethin' to build up yer appetite for dinner." He smirked.

Jasper sighed. He knew his Sergeants wouldn't give it up, and he looked back to Onyx, who was brushing the dust off her legs. She walked over to the group, the last to join as she stood there with her hands on her hips. "What's next?"

Studying her, he noticed that though she had broken a bit of a sweat, she still seemed alert and attentive. Before any words came out of his mouth, Tarren's stupid voice rang out, "We're bettin' you could e'en take our Lieuten't here, girl."

"I don't see why not. I could use a challenge," she teased, getting a laugh from the group. This was good. They seemed to enjoy her presence, even though she wasn't one to call attention to herself. And truly, when she wasn't focused on training, there was an easygoing, pleasant energy about her. He wondered if any of his soldiers saw him the same way but pushed that thought to the side. It didn't matter. He was their Lieutenant first, and a friend second, if that.

All looks shifted to Jasper. Taking a deep breath, he nodded and walked with her to the spot where his men had spent the day grappling. Those large eyes watched him as he turned to face her. He felt a bit uncomfortable—he'd never really fought a woman before. Would it be any different than fighting a man? Even though she was just a couple of inches shorter than him, she was slimmer than the men. Somehow she had managed to use that to her advantage with the others and would undoubtedly do so with him as well.

The deliberation took away from his focus, and he almost missed her shift just past him. The Lieutenant bent his knee before she could kick the back of it, gripping around her waist with his arm and pivoting behind her to try and wrap his other arm around her neck. She must've intuited it, however, because she whirled her way out of his grasp and stayed close to his body, coming around *his* back. Onyx grabbed both his shoulders, this time successfully kicking him in the back of his other knee as she pulled his shoulders back and down, snaking her arm around his neck as he fell into her grip. "Is that all you got?" she taunted in a quickened breath, earning a few whistles from the guys.

Jasper smirked. She had gotten cocky, not doing enough to knock him off his balance or to choke him. Grabbing the arm around his neck with both hands and pulling it down, he brought his elbows behind his back before she had the chance to react. He gripped onto her forearm with one hand and spun himself around to place a foot behind her feet, tripping her backward as he pushed on her torso with his shoulder and took her down. But she held on tightly, her weight bringing him down with her. A cloud of dust billowed around them as the two landed in the dirt, his face just inches from hers, feeling her heavy breaths. She was pinned down by his weight and had no way to escape it now.

Their eyes locked again, and his breath caught as she slowly stopped struggling. The dust had settled by the time he realized they had been locked in that position for a couple of seconds too long, with him breathing heavily on top of her and her doing nothing but watching. Finally, she smacked the ground a couple of times with her free hand and the Lieutenant released her. He looked away sheepishly and nodded to his men before getting up and moving off to the side, clearing his throat and avoiding eye contact with her.

"Good work. You're all dismissed for the day." The men nodded, and he could feel Onyx's eyes on him, but he didn't dare glance at her again as he walked away, readjusting the sleeves on his arms.

Regardless of how they initially met, he couldn't deny that she knew exactly what she was doing. The King had said she was a huntress, and Jasper didn't doubt that. She was dangerous, no matter how likable, pretty, or adept she was. And based on what he saw, he wasn't entirely convinced she only had experience with animals.

FOURTEEN

ANGHEL

———

The throne room's white pointed arches, lining the ceiling with curved brown wood for contrast, loomed above Anghel as he wove between the beveled brown columns underneath. Blue banners with the Padaurean blackbird decorated the walls with armored statues interspersed throughout the room as if they were guards standing there, watching over it.

Natural light filled the hall, entering from the tall, rectangular windows. On their stair-like sills sat a gray-bearded man with a letter in his hand. Edon was one of Duke Aurel's messengers with the cursive blue *A* sewed into his shirt underneath the Padaurean blackbird sigil.

After pouring both of them a drink, Anghel sat down on the steps, leaning against the wall on the other side of the windowsill. He took a moment to observe the man's upright posture, finding amusement in the tension he could see in the man's shoulders.

Based on what he knew about the Duke, he wasn't surprised. The amount of perfection and strict organization demanded by him, he imagined, would be enough to keep anyone in his service on their toes, even if he was effective at his post.

The man shook his head vigorously as Anghel placed the cup in front of him, putting up a hand. "My Prince, you are far too kind. I should be fetching you something to quench your thirst."

"Nonsense, my good man," the Prince chuckled, shifting the cup on the sill. "You're not here to see me, and I should try to be good company while my father finishes his business."

"He does seem like a busy man. I would hate to rush anything of his or be of any inconvenience to him, and I imagine you are also a very active and busy person, who should not be frivolous with his time with one such as me…" The man trailed off.

Right. Anghel took a deep breath as he drank some of the wine. From their limited interactions, Edon seemed the type to constantly feel the need to prove himself in intellect as he got older and physically weaker, wasting his breath on long words and even longer sentences for what a few words would suffice to say. It was hard for Anghel not to chuckle at the silliness of it all.

"What brings you here, Edon?" the Prince asked. "I imagine, coming all the way from the northmost province, you must have something of import to tell. Any idea what that might be?"

The man anxiously fiddled with the parchment in his hand, but it had remained sealed, and he didn't show any interest in opening it up. Anghel sighed. Even now, at twenty-two, he was treated as an authority on the surface, but when it came to something of substance, he was still barely a political apprentice to his father. "So nothing significant happened?"

The messenger sighed. "If I were to speculate, I would say that perhaps it is about the wedding of my Duke's eldest to Prince Merek, royal heir of Apasia."

Anghel's eyebrows furrowed in confusion. He couldn't figure out why it had caught him off guard, but it did. The most influential Duke in the kingdom, a longtime friend of his father's, was marrying off his daughter to the Prince of *another* kingdom, rather than his own? Their capital might have been slightly closer to the estate than that of Padaure's, but had the Duke even pondered staying loyal to his own?

Edon raised those grayed eyebrows upon catching his reaction, and despite Anghel's own attempts to replace his expression with a neutral one, the Prince had betrayed his reaction already. "My Prince, please take no offense and accept my sincerest apologies. Perhaps I should not have said anything. I knew it was blessed by your own father as a way to strengthen our Apasian alliance. I had thought he might have mentioned it to you since the last time he had corresponded with Duke Aurel—"

"He had not," Anghel replied softly, looking down and taking a sip of the drink. Why was he upset? He couldn't even recall if he had ever met the Duke's daughter. If he had, it would have been at a very young age, too young to remember anything distinct about her, but the idea that his father was blessing marriages behind his back bothered him for some reason.

Anghel admittedly hadn't given marriage too much thought, pushing the idea back as a future concern every time his father brought it up, so perhaps he shouldn't have been too surprised at the notion. After all, he was still young. He had explored most of the unmarried women in the Capital and had his fun with those from other cities before his father stopped taking him to estate visits. But there was still so much to experience—places to explore, women to meet—before he would be tied down to this boring royal life forever. Right?

"It is good to see you again, my dear Edon," his father's voice boomed, echoing in the room. Both men looked up to see the silver-and-black-haired King stroll confidently toward them, his gait regal and self-assured as always.

Immediately, the messenger sprung up and bowed. "My King." Anghel tried not to roll his eyes.

Miran graciously smiled at them. "I hope I am not interrupting anything."

"Not at all," Anghel muttered, "we were just having a chat."

"Oh, dear," the King chuckled, turning to Edon. "Forgive my son, I had not caught him up on everything yet."

"Of course, Your Majesty." Edon bowed.

Miran faced his son, placing a hand on his arm and squeezing once. Anghel remained stiff and seated, though he looked into his father's lavender eyes. "Would you mind leaving me here to chat about political matters with Edon? I know these things can bore you, but I will tell you all about it soon."

The Prince swallowed, trying not to reveal his frustration, especially in the face of a guest. "Of course, Father." He smiled falsely. "I need to go pay Jasper a visit anyway." His father nodded, and Anghel got up, nodding in acknowledgment to Edon before stepping out of the throne room. He wondered what else his father was keeping from him.

Strolling out of the castle onto the bridge in his more casual town clothes, he admired how the sinking sun cast a golden hue upon the red roofs that filled the city below him. Taking in a breath of the fresh air was a relief after spending all day holed up in the castle, acting as both his father's half-assed political apprentice and clueless son. Unfortunately, this was his royal life, and eventually, this would be his full-time job whenever his father decided to give up the throne and stop treating him like a child.

He continued winding down toward the soldiers' chambers, entering the spacious, dusty courtyard through the large, open gate at the forefront. The men had grouped up, chattering as they put away their weapons in the bins and racks under a covered hall on the west side of the courtyard. Just another evening, it seemed.

Or was it? He saw an unfamiliar figure and walked toward it. Her slender body was covered in dark clothing that hugged her form and seemed to cover all but her hands, neck, and face with the occasional patches of dust that she hadn't seemed to brush off yet.

Tracing the curves of her body, his eyes traveled up her hips that funneled into an hourglass waist and up to her delicate features, revealed by the brown hair that was pulled out of her face. She walked gracefully with a quiet but distinct presence, complemented by her long legs and toned arms, with a perfect arch in her lower back that flattered the shape of an ample—

"Maiden's Mug as usual?" The Prince turned to see Tarren walking toward him and gave him a quick nod, one that was reciprocated by the Sergeant before he walked out through the gates.

Anghel's gaze returned to the woman. The other men seemed to pay her no attention for some reason as she floated across the grassy area on the east side of the courtyard toward one of the doors to the chambers. His curiosity got the better of him, and he found himself following her into the lantern-lit hallway. She glanced back just enough to reveal the side of her face before abruptly picking up her pace.

Turning into one of the rooms, she tried to slam the door, but Anghel caught it right before she was able to close it. "Haven't seen you here before," he said, and she stopped resisting. Inviting himself into the room, he walked through the doorway and swiveled to face her. "If you're waiting for one of the soldiers, you'll be sorely disappointed. You'd be better off with someone else." He winked at her.

The woman scoffed, crossing her arms and narrowing her eyes. "That's not why I'm here." She had a foreign accent, one he hadn't heard before, but combined with the sound of her voice, it was almost musical.

Anghel walked over to her, feeling the stern intensity of her gaze on him that didn't leave, even as he brushed her upper arm. He remained just inches away from her as he looked down into her dark, scrutinizing eyes. She was a feisty one. He leaned over to whisper softly in her ear, "It can be now."

She stiffened and even flinched as he reached to brush a stray hair out of her face. Placing a hand on his chest, she pushed him away a little bit. "Please trust me when I say you would not want to try anything."

He grinned. "You're a dangerous one? It would explain the getup. You don't dress like the others."

The woman looked a bit confused. "I seem to have the wrong body for dressing like the men."

Anghel chuckled. She had a sense of humor, it seemed, despite her serious face, her doe-like eyes still watching him carefully. "A blessing for us all," he replied, his glance trailing down her body before looking back at her face as his arm swirled around her waist. "Perhaps you could bless me a little bit more."

Swinging her elbow into his face, she struck him in his nose and left eye. Before he could figure out what was happening, the woman's leg moved behind his and she pushed her torso into him. When he hit the floor, she placed one knee on his chest, her body weight keeping him from getting up. He hadn't expected her to be so strong. "Couldn't say I didn't warn you," she said.

"What's going on here?" The Prince heard his brother's voice as Jasper entered through the doorway. He could've sworn he saw a bit of bemusement on the Lieutenant's face, but it shifted to concern.

The woman looked back up to him. "Seems that one of yours didn't get the message about me. He followed me into my room."

Jasper glanced back and forth between the two of them and motioned with his chin for her to move off. As she complied, he extended a hand to Anghel, who accepted it and let his brother help him up. "I see you've finally met the Prince," the Lieutenant said.

Her eyes widened, and she looked at Anghel in shock. "I-I had no idea—"

"What?" the Prince interrupted, brushing himself off.

"Anghel," his brother said calmly, gesturing toward the woman. "This is Onyx. She's our newest recruit."

"I've never heard of a woman joining the Guard," he mused.

She started to say something, but Jasper interrupted her with a comforting hand on her shoulder.

"Please do forgive my brother," he told her before turning back to Anghel. "Father met her recently and brought her back. What you just saw her do is nothing compared to what she's capable of." The Prince could've sworn he saw her cheeks flush a light pink at the compliment, but it was hard to detect in this lighting, and Jasper continued, apparently not noticing. "One of his terms was that she is not to involve herself with the soldiers here."

Anghel opened his mouth to ask why, but he doubted they would know the real reason. He bowed his head in shame. "My apologies, my lady. Communication, at least with me, is not my father's strong point."

One of her eyebrows arched apprehensively, but she nodded in acknowledgment. "My apologies to you as well, my Prince."

A tense pause ensued, and he decided to be the one to break it again. "Perhaps I should leave. Fancy meeting you— although I regret that it wasn't on more... polite terms." And with a nod, he walked out, leaving the two in the room.

Wiping his nose, he noticed a trail of blood on his hand from it and chuckled to himself. The Prince wasn't used to rejection. In fact, he wasn't used to women *not* jumping at such opportunities with him, much less tackling him without stripping their clothes off. His natural magnetism was something he'd inherited from his mother, along with her blond hair and taste for experience. But perhaps this experience, in particular, was a warning not to follow in her footsteps.

FIFTEEN

OTRA

The square was filled with a sort of vibrance even in the day, merchants offering anything ranging from shiny, bright red apples to handmade, fine green linens. The setting sun shone over everyone and everything in the crowded Lebirosi marketplace as they were getting ready for another night of the festival, and Otra kept her hood up to mask the dark curls she had tucked back.

Watching the little children playing and the adults who looked at them adoringly, she couldn't help but feel like she was in some sort of dream. She was even envious of those children, able to run around and toss fruit toward one another without a care in the world.

She thought of her life before the Phoenix had taken her in. Back in those days, she used to have to knife-fight other street orphans for just a bite of an apple, wincing at the thought of the resulting wounds she used to have to dress in the alleyways with what rags or leaves she could gather.

As the sun began to dip, she couldn't help but wonder what was going on in the city and how its citizens seemed so happy with one another. It was a peaceful place, and perhaps part of the life that filled it was due to the excitement about the festival, but how was it prosperous enough to have *everyone* seem content and happy? Even more so, how could the city afford to withstand what would be weeks of celebration?

Otra hoped to find out. After all, it was part of the reason she was here, to learn more of Midstad's secrets and how the Lebirosi maintained such a quality of life for its citizens. Once the Phoenix expanded its influence enough, they could use such secrets to keep building that better world that her superiors would always go on about.

The most beautiful thing in the world is how much potential there is, her leader had once said, *and the ugly part of it is the lack of guarantee in how much of it, if any, is fulfilled.* Perhaps this place, once Otra found the chinks in its armor and learned of its secrets, would help the Phoenix erase that ugly part. She smiled at the thought of the Continent with Lumina in control, where children everywhere could run around with screams of laughter under a peaceful regime, not just here.

"Well, if it isn't my favorite little dancer," a familiar voice said. She turned to see Vitor from the night before, and heat rose in her cheeks. Her breath caught in her mouth, and she froze, her eyes darting around to try and find the best route to escape, wondering if it was worth it to even talk to him.

Wait—what better way to learn of the Allied Cities' secrets, than through someone intimately acquainted with them?

He interrupted her thoughts, offering his arm. "May I join you?"

She took a deep breath, deciding not to give up *too* easily. He seemed to like the way she toyed with him. "You really don't give up, do you?"

He chuckled, his warm brown eyes looking at her with— did she dare think—admiration? "What can I say? I'm almost as stubborn as you are." He winked.

Rolling her eyes, she took his arm, pretending not to notice how firm it was as they walked together through the cobblestone streets of the city and approached the music that had started playing.

"Besides, you are rather wonderful to dance with, and I was hoping to find you and perhaps do that again tonight."

"Perhaps a little dance couldn't hurt," she replied coyly.

"In fact, I would dance with you until you decide to tell me your true name, my lady."

She laughed. "I wouldn't consider myself a lady."

"I would. And you're changing the subject."

"Is that a challenge?"

"Only if you accept."

She laughed. "You have no idea what you're bringing yourself into."

He turned toward her, pulling her close and locking eyes with her again. "I'm curious enough to find out." Otra felt as if he were looking through her and analyzing her to her core, although she wasn't sure if he knew what he was seeing.

She felt a light fluttering in her chest as his arm lightly grasped her waist and her hand settled on his shoulder, their other hands clasping together. He instantly began to lead her into a new dance, fluidly spinning and moving in perfect cadence. She found herself freely smiling and opening up a bit more. Maybe it wouldn't be the worst thing to play with him a bit.

The people and the night passed by, but it felt like only seconds by the time the band ceased to play. The barkeeps nearby were forcing out both them and the other couple who had stayed just a little bit too long. They laughed as they walked out onto the street, which was sparse by now, in the dead of night.

Their hands were still clasped together, to her surprise, but neither made an effort to let go. She didn't mind the feeling, and what was the harm in leaving it at that? Perhaps he felt the same. A shame that she might have to kill such a nice thing.

"So how is it that the city can afford to keep the spirits so high?"

"What do you mean by that?" Vitor asked in return, his eyes on her.

She found herself looking away, idly observing the taller clay buildings that lined the street they walked down. "Everything here seems so... prosperous," she replied.

"Something you're not used to?" he asked in a not-so-subtle solicitation of information from her. But she knew how to play these games better than he did, even if he thought he could read her better than most. She was determined to get him to reveal more than she would.

"Something many cities to this day have trouble with. As someone who works for the law, I figured you might have a unique perspective." Playing up his confidence with compliments was a sure way to get any man to reveal more. Regardless of who it was, they all worked the same, and if need be, she could give up more to get more.

Or did they? He smirked at her. "It's kind of you to say, my lady. We Lebirosi just look for the prosperity of our citizens first. With our Council as the highest rank, we reject the idea of royal families to hoard all the wealth of the region."

Hmm. Otra had gotten a bit, but this was information she could extract from any local. This man worked for the law.

He *had* to know more than that, and she was determined to pull it out of him, bit by bit.

But she couldn't deny that they might have the right idea. While she didn't mind the thought of her leader as a monarch, she could see how their own council of Generals and advisors she surrounded herself with might be able to emulate Lebirosi ideas to ensure the prosperity their leader always talked about and promised. Otra made a mental note to herself to talk to Lumina about it after learning more, hoping it wouldn't be too far above her rank to do so.

She found herself following him to an inn, where he left a coin on the front counter and led her into a room lit by a lantern with pretty red sheets neatly tucked over the bed. Vitor gently closed the door behind him as she began to remove her hood and her dress, exposing her bare skin and undergarments. She'd been in this situation enough where she knew what to do, and experience told her to lie in the bed as she watched him take off his shoes and shirt, exposing more of his bronze skin and a bare, well-built chest.

As he walked over to her, she gazed upon his face. Now with it better lit, she could see his strong jawline, smooth skin, and long eyelashes. She reflected on the night, of how much fun they had together, before realizing she might actually be deflowered if she didn't kill him soon enough. But which was she more inclined to do?

Perhaps she would actually give herself up to this one. He was far too valuable a resource to kill before anything could happen, as she had a habit of doing with the others. Her leader's words echoed again in her head. *You must not forget, child, that men pride themselves so much on their strength, their wit, their wisdom—yet never learn not to sacrifice it all once a woman opens her legs to him.* It was time.

He lay beside her on the bed and brought his arm around her, cupping his free hand around her face. "You're even more beautiful right now."

She smiled, her heart skipping a beat, and let him pull her in to kiss her.

She had a hard time getting over how different this was from what she was used to. Rather than forceful or overzealous, this one was soft and even intimate? Otra was shocked to find his hands not haphazardly wandering around her body, but rather gently caressing her back, and even more surprised to find him pulling away to kiss her on the forehead before leaning back on the pillows.

Seeming to note her confusion, he chuckled, his fingers slowly running through her hair and tucking it behind her ear. This was... nice? Strange? She wasn't quite sure how to characterize it, but this man definitely knew what he was doing. He was purposely holding back so she'd want more, just as she'd done to countless men before.

"My apologies. I don't go very far with women if I don't know their name," he teased. "You're more than welcome to join me in sleeping here, but it won't be in the way you may expect." He winked at her, and she couldn't help but let out a laugh as she rested her head on his chest, staring up at the ceiling.

"I thought I already told you," she replied slyly, "is that not good enough for you?"

He let out a laugh. "You're not the first pretty liar I've encountered. We both know I have the capacity to unravel your lies as quickly as you can spin them."

"Do we now?"

"And I think it's something you're not used to. Actually, I think it scares the living hell out of you."

She laughed at his statement, not wanting to admit he was right. He definitely was smarter than the average man she normally seduced and had more of a mind than most—one that was able to keep up with her, as if they were doing a separate, delicate dance. But Otra needed to win this game. She never lost, and she refused to start now, even as she felt the slow rise and fall of his chest. She matched her breathing to his and slowly closed her eyes as they both let sleep catch up to them.

SIXTEEN

CARNELO

The woods were filled with a light mist as Carnelo treaded through the forest for this week's hunt, clutching his handmade bow and arrows. Moving quietly and deliberately, he hovered on the balls of his feet as he stepped over twigs and fallen branches, listening for his potential prey.

He never liked it when it got this misty. It reminded him of pieces of his past that he preferred not to think about. Yet they intruded now, as he reflexively rubbed his neck and felt the scars that covered that along with most of his chest.

The smoke still filled the village when Carnelo woke up to the deafening quiet. Pain shot up through his chest and neck, and he looked down to find gashes and burnt skin as tears welled up in his eyes. Despite the silence, the deafening screams and crackling of burning buildings among which he'd passed out echoed in his head, and he kept seeing the purple flames that had enveloped the tiny mountain village.

Turning over, he screamed as he looked through an open doorway to see a charred carcass burnt almost beyond recognition underneath a tree that had fallen through the straw roof. He almost wished he hadn't been able to recognize it—the form of his mother, mouth open in a silent, endless scream.

He heard a rustle and saw a young buck gently slinking through the trees just sixty feet ahead of him with half-grown antlers and a light sienna coat. Mimicking the deer's motions, he kept his eyes trained on the animal as it stopped and looked around. Shifting behind a tree, he was just barely able to escape its line of sight as it surveyed the area.

If this thing started running, it would be near-impossible to catch. Luckily, it was upwind and turned away from Carnelo. As the animal continued through, the man silently slid the arrow onto the string, pulling the end to his ear as he stretched it back.

Eyeing the buck carefully, he aimed for its center first and then shifted his direction up, trying his best for a clean shot at the spinal cord. He could sense the animal's apprehension, and he manipulated its energy to diminish its alertness to the point where the deer barely reacted when the string snapped back to its position as he released the arrow.

As the animal collapsed with a short, deep groan, Carnelo jogged over to make sure it had stopped breathing. He had gotten the shot right this time, he noticed. Its entire body was twitching. As he stood over the paralyzed animal, he released another arrow to the heart to put it out of its misery. Cutting it open, he pulled out its guts to make it easier to carry, leaving its insides as food for the other animals in the forest. He grunted as he lifted the animal over his shoulders and began his walk back home.

The forest was a vast and lonely place. Little Carnelo wished he were back home, but what was there for him? His parents, as with all of his friends, had been burned to ashes, and his brother was nowhere to be found, likely also burnt beyond recognition. It was all gone now, and what was the point in staying? To be eaten by the wolves?

His chest pain had numbed, something he'd have to force himself to ignore if he was to get himself out of this place. Yet the pain inside it hadn't stopped; it only grew as he stepped farther and farther away from the ruins of home into the darkening forest, where he would encounter who-knew-what.

"Decen' catch, son," his stepfather said, approving of the carcass they'd tied up behind their small cottage.

Carnelo nodded, tightening the last knot.

"Y' always know how t' get th' best ones."

"Thanks, Tata," Carnelo replied with a halfhearted smile, brushing dark, wavy hair out of his eyes. Looking up, he saw that the sun had just set, and that meant that his old friend Atora would be home, reading in her room by the lantern light, having just finished dinner.

"I've gotta go see a friend," he told the older man, who inattentively nodded, heading inside to grab the knives to skin the animal. Carnelo darted around the small house, quickening his pace as he headed toward the stone castle.

Duke Aurel's castle was small compared to others, at least based on what Atora had told him from her experiences, but it still towered over the village underneath it. Stone by stone, he scaled the erratic wall of a nearby two-story inn and jumped onto its roof before leaping onto the roof of another building nearby, and another, until he was just a couple of yards underneath the right window.

Gingerly, he took the same steps he did every time, placing a foot out to one of the ledges and sticking his other foot in a crack just above. Using the latter foot to propel himself up and grasp the windowsill, he pulled himself up and over, lifting his legs over and sitting on the stone edge to catch his breath.

There were probably more convenient ways to reach her, but he wasn't sure how the Duke would feel about his daughter being close friends with a commoner or whether he'd be allowed inside. Besides, he kind of enjoyed the climbing and roof-running it took for him to reach the window, and it felt natural to him by now.

"Zbura!" Atora exclaimed in a loud whisper, and he couldn't help but grin at the charming nickname only she had for him. It meant "the flier" in an old book she'd read, and she always said that the way he made his way up to her window was so graceful it was as if he had flown to her. While he definitely considered that debatable, he appreciated the compliment every time, especially coming from her sweet, pleasant voice.

She walked over and hugged him, and he embraced her in return, delighting in her smaller, delicate frame in his arms and her head against his chest.

"Is everything alright?" he asked, concerned. While she was the affectionate type, he noticed that she held on a bit tighter than usual. He felt her nod as he ran his fingers through her hair to soothe her.

"I'm just missing Letta." She sighed when she pulled back, the fading light from her window filling up those clear blue eyes. "She left for Apasia, and she's getting married in a week. I'm just not sure if I'm ready to say goodbye yet."

He took a deep breath. If Letta was already getting married, that meant that it wouldn't be very long before there was a similar plan for Atora. She was only younger by a year, and the Duke wasn't known for his patience. "Is it really goodbye? She's still your sister."

She walked over to her bed, and he followed, both of them sitting to face each other. "I know, and we *said* we'd write, but we *have* grown apart since we were young. We just like different things, and I feel like I'm going to lose her completely. I don't want to be just some random face to her that she sees at the occasional royal event, if at all."

Carnelo wrapped his arms around her, hugging her tightly again, one hand tracing her upper back to soothe her. He could see why she was so conflicted. From what he knew, Letta was the more reserved sort and rather pompous even. Apasia sounded like the perfect place for her, but she was still Atora's sister. "Don't say that. I'm sure you two'll be able t' talk more than that. How'd she say goodbye?"

Atora sniffled. The lanterns in her room were dim, and it was dark enough that Carnelo hadn't seen that she'd been crying, but he mentally kicked himself for not noticing sooner. "She gave me a book—her favorite one."

"Have you been reading that?" he asked, trying not to let his heart break from the tears he felt on his shoulder.

The girl nodded. "It's not bad, actually. Maybe I can use it as an excuse to talk with her more at the wedding."

"I'm sure she'd love that." He gave her a tight squeeze, reaching up to wipe away the tears from her face. These conversations in the shadows of her canopied bed, just hearing about her day and speaking from the heart in the light of the moonbeams that trickled through that tall window with the rounded top, were what he looked forward to most. He always had since they had met about ten years ago.

She laid her head on his shoulder, and he took in the negative energy that had been afflicting her, sensing her anxiety and sadness before diminishing it. He was always happy to see the same effect of his energy manipulation, her predictably sighing as if breathing everything out, and the tension leaving her body.

"Thanks for coming," she said. "I don't know what it is about you, but you always calm me down."

Brushing back a strand of thick brown hair that escaped from the bundle she had tucked behind her ear, he smiled and gave her a friendly kiss on the forehead. "Of course. Where else would I want to be?"

SEVENTEEN

CITRINA

Taking another sip of the brandy in her small leather pouch, Citrina brought her knife by her ear, aiming at the pinewood target she had stolen and brought out of the yard into the outskirts, in the green space that separated the building from the forest. After all, it was the end of the week, and the other soldiers liked bringing women to their chambers. The least she could do was let them have fun and not scare off the other girls, no matter how much she missed having her own fun.

Despite being the only woman, she felt she had adjusted quite nicely. She still felt the glances the others would sneak, but she couldn't blame them. With the exception of the few hours a week of free time, they were used to being surrounded only by other men. They'd probably stare at Citrina even if she were a one-toothed hag, but she appreciated that they still treated her with the same respect due to any other soldier, as instructed. She could focus on refining her skills, both in and out of training.

The only instance of note thus far had been her brief interaction with the Prince. She had heard tales here and there of his libido, but based on her assessment of him, she couldn't see why he was so successful besides the fact that he was royalty. He was somewhat attractive, sure, but not anything special, not like—

"*Interesting* idea, to say the least," a voice said as she flung the knife, and she turned her head to see the Lieutenant as she heard the *thud* of a successful landing. He had been particularly quiet, though even with her diverted attention, she thought she should have heard him. So she wondered how long he had been standing there, watching her.

"Figured I might challenge myself." She shrugged, trying to play off her surprise.

"That's a hell of a way to challenge yourself," he replied, glancing at the leather flask in her hand.

Citrina lifted it with a half-smile. "Want a sip?"

He hesitated, glancing between her and the drink she was offering before politely shaking his head. "I don't believe knives and alcohol mix very well together."

She let out a shallow laugh before capping the flask and putting it away in the folds of her clothing. "Speak for yourself."

"I beg your pardon?"

Lifting another knife from her sheath, her gaze returned to the target as she pulled her arm back again. "If that's what you think, that suggests you haven't learned how to hold your alcohol well."

"I would disagree."

"You can do that." She nodded, releasing the knife and landing it dead center, just above the previous blade she'd thrown. "While I try to train so I can handle myself, no matter my state."

"Or the state of your surroundings, I take it."

She nodded, before wondering how well he could see her in the night. "Why else would I be out training in the dark?"

"Perhaps the training doesn't pose enough of a challenge to you," he mused.

She turned to him, her eyes widening. "Th-that's not what I mean—"

Jasper smiled at her, raising a hand as he took a couple of steps toward her and surveyed the environment. She had a slightly easier time seeing him now in the beams of moonlight that escaped between the clouds. "It is. Don't worry about it. I feel the same way. I often find myself out here as well." Crossing his arms, he laughed and looked down. "In fact, that's what the Sergeants like to tease me for."

That explains a lot. Citrina walked over to the target to pull out the blades. How else would he have found himself in charge of the Guard at such a young age?

Twirling a knife between her fingers, she strolled back toward him and held out the handle as an offer. "Might as well embrace it." She grinned.

He let out a small chuckle and gracefully slipped the blade into his hand, observing the handle and the curve of her black blade before turning his body to face the target. After bringing the knife by his ear, the smile disappeared into an expression of focus as he flung it, landing just off-center.

"That the best you've got, sir?" Citrina teased.

He turned his head, the corners of his mouth quirking up. "Let's see you do better, miss," he retorted, stepping back and offering her the spot.

"Gladly." This attempt seemed to land just a hair off from the center, right next to his.

"Not *much* better," he joked, walking over to pull them out. As his back was turned, she observed his solid form. Each step was assertive yet strangely regal. After all, he had grown up surrounded by royals, and it was obvious their style had rubbed off on him in his walk and his speech, despite the rugged nature of his position.

Jasper studied the blades upon walking back to her. "May I ask where you got these from? They don't look like the ones we use in training."

"They aren't," she told him. "They're mine. I use them on my hunts."

"Which one was used on the infamous boar that Miran keeps telling me about?"

She smirked, pointing out the one he held in his left hand. "That one was used to cut the tendon. Had to weaken it before I could deliver the finishing blow."

Looking back at her, he did a playful half-bow. "I am so honored," he said, very obviously trying not to laugh as she did.

Handing the blade back to her as they ceased laughing, Jasper continued, "Tell me, are boars the only thing you hunt?"

"Of course not. It depends on what people are willing to pay me for—foxes, stags, those kinds of things."

"Mhm," he nodded, crossing his arms again. "Do they pay you more for people?"

Citrina was taken aback by the accusation. Of course, she had twenty-eight tallies on her forearm so far, but she hadn't revealed that part of her to anybody in Padaure, not even him. He had no reason to suspect that she was any sort of assassin, or at least, she thought so. "I'm afraid I don't know what you're talking about."

He scoffed. "Forgive me. I just find it hard to believe that hunting animals alone gives you the technique I've seen in you."

She swallowed. He wasn't fooled. He was definitely onto her. But how? Regardless, she had to think on her feet. "You're right," she admitted, putting away her blades. "It doesn't."

"May I ask what does, then?"

Hesitating, she looked down and took a deep breath before looking back up at him. "Not all of us grew up lucky enough to have the *choice* to learn how to fight," she answered softly, remembering the street-rat story she'd led Miran to believe.

Jasper's expression changed to one of surprise and pity, and he looked down at his feet as if he regretted asking the question. "Oh," he replied, and she dignified it only with a nod and a blank expression, happy that she'd gotten away with such a surface-level answer. It wasn't a complete lie, even if she had enjoyed growing up learning from Lumina and her other associates.

"I don't blame you for asking," she comforted him, placing a hand on his exposed upper arm and pretending not to notice how solid it was. "I know you only want what's best for your people."

Looking back at her, he nodded. "I'm glad you understand, and it *did* seem a bit strange in timing, what with..." The Lieutenant trailed off with a shrug, but she knew exactly what he was referring to.

She nodded, mirroring him. "Exactly. Just... interesting timing." There was a bit of an awkward pause, filled in only by the rustle of leaves in the forest and cicadas buzzing off in the distance, before Citrina decided to interrupt it with a thought that had just occurred. "Have you told—"

Jasper shook his head. "I doubt you would still be here practicing if I did."

She let out a sigh of relief and raised her hand to run through her braided hair, puzzled. "I appreciate that. But I must ask, why didn't you?"

He glanced at the target before returning his gaze to hers. "I wanted to see what you were capable of first."

Citrina watched his face. "And?"

The Lieutenant's lips curved into another small smile. "I was impressed. The King was right. You do make a valuable contribution."

"That's very kind of you to say, sir," she said, bowing her head.

Only when she looked back up into his eyes did she realize how physically close they had become. She could see the stubble that had started to shadow his face and the moonlight leaking into his eyes. "You can just call me Jasper when the others aren't around. No need for formalities," he said in a soft, amicable tone. "It'd actually feel more... normal."

Citrina nodded, her breath caught in her throat. He looked at her intently, as if he were going to say something, but then looked down again. "I should go," he said. "Perhaps you should get some rest as well."

She agreed, and as he started to walk away, she realized she'd forgotten to thank him for his discretion. "Jasper," she said, impulsively grasping his forearm. He let out a quick gasp as he looked at her hand. She followed his gaze and saw she had accidentally pulled down the wraps he always wore, revealing darkened skin with white scars lacing it, and—*were they glowing*?

Yanking her hand away, they watched as the glow slowly began to fade. Looking back up to his face, she saw that he was also staring at his forearm incredulously, turning it over and softly brushing it with his own fingers.

"I'm sorry," she said, running a hand through her hair. "I… I just wanted to thank you. For being so kind and not saying anything, that is."

The Lieutenant nodded, avoiding eye contact with her as he swiftly pulled the wraps back up. "It was a mistake on both of our parts." She could've sworn she heard him add as he walked away, "Even if a nice one."

He disappeared around the building, looking to go toward the castle, and she waited a few moments for him to go on his own before deciding to walk to the target and begin carrying it back to the soldiers' courtyard. Her mind raced. What just happened? Why did he have those scars? Why were they *glowing*? The patterning was too unique, too familiar.

Returning to her room, in the glow of the lanterns and the faint sounds of women's exaggerated gasping, she locked her door and began to remove her own clothing. In the mirror, she observed the dark purpled skin that covered her entire upper back, laced with white scarring that looked like haphazard scratches. *So familiar.*

EIGHTEEN

———

The blonde maiden had been both excited and nervous all week, pacing back and forth in the tiny excuse for a room she lived in. Barely three paces from the opening that served as a door to her makeshift cot against the wall, barely three paces back. She found it hard to sleep, making checklists in her mind of everything she'd need to bring, not that she needed much other than the rags she called clothing, the few coins she'd strung together from begging, and some food for the road.

Life went on in the village, but there seemed to be even less life in it now. She could only imagine how wondrous and fascinating the world outside of it would be and how exciting it would be to explore the unknown with Petyr. The necklace hadn't left her neck, although she kept it hidden under her ragged clothing.

There was a skip in her step that day as she approached the market in the square. She was only sixteen, and her savings were incredibly modest, but she had enough to buy a thing or two that she might need.

As she purchased a loaf of bread from the baker, she heard shouts. "That's the boy!"

Turning around, she saw a rush of guards, and—was that the lord's son?—but couldn't see who they had captured or what was going on. She was short enough that the crowd blocked her view, and she didn't realize who it was until they took him up to the gallows with bound hands and feet.

They tightened a noose around Petyr's neck for all to see as the lord's son confidently and deliberately made his way up the steps, coiling and uncoiling the nine-tails in his hand as the guards ripped off their new prisoner's shirt. The royal seemed to relish the gallows—it was prominent in the square as an example for all townsfolk.

Movement seemed to still in the square as all eyes moved to the royal. He glanced at the waiting crowd with a grin, the glint in his eyes betraying his anticipation. The whole town knew he was always ready to deliver punishment. Commoners knew better than to step out of line, in fear of what he'd do. One could only imagine his delight upon finding someone who actually dared to break the law.

Petyr's eyes seemed to search the crowd and stopped when they met hers. "Run," he mouthed. She shook her head, tears welling up in her eyes. Sorrow fell upon his face, and he mouthed again to her, "Please."

She knew there was nothing either of them could do now. Even if she ran to return the necklace, it wouldn't matter. He'd still be punished, and perhaps she would too. Petyr wouldn't want that, nor for her to see whatever was about to happen to him. But the shock set in, and she couldn't bring herself to look away, either, as the lashes began to fall. She couldn't believe they had taken him away from her already, so quickly and so easily.

Forcing a small grimace, she mouthed to him, "I love you," hoping he could see her from this distance. Her hand brushed the cloth on her neck that concealed the necklace. Her heart raced. She had never said that to anyone before, but she knew it'd be her last chance to say it to him.

It seemed that Petyr noticed because his eyes lit up. He grinned like a madman as he took in every last moment of her, much to the dismay of the lord's son, who looked out into the crowd in confusion. It was typical of Petyr, spiting royals even as he was being punished, lash after lash delivered on his bare back.

Time seemed to slow down as the girl watched blood trickle down his skinny body, flowing to cover every square inch of his otherwise beautiful tan skin. The exposed muscle seemed to splash and squish with every additional hit.

It was a horror to watch, seeing him whipped to a pulp for all to see, made even worse by the seemingly endless energy of his punisher. She wondered if he would ever stop.

Eventually, he did cease, letting out a frustrated sigh and muttering to himself, probably because Petyr didn't yell out like most would. She couldn't help but think what a strange sight it probably was to everyone else—a skinny young boy covered in his own blood, delivering a tired yet cocky smile to a grown, sweaty man as if to say, "Is that all you got?"

The man didn't seem too happy with the young rascal's last act of rebellion, and he stormed over to the nearby lever.

The blonde maiden looked back up at Petyr's face, and his eyes met hers. His deranged grin had been replaced by an expression of pure sorrow. She had seen these kinds of things before, of course, and she knew pain was no stranger to her or Petyr. They'd lived their entire lives as street rats and child beggars, kicked at by strangers.

But the pain they now shared was a new kind. All she could do was watch the humanity of the love of her life reduced with *every new gash that had cut deeper into his flesh. All she could see were the spasms that took over as the floor fell out from under him.*

Perhaps the worst part was that his eyes never left hers, even as the life left his. As his body went limp, the voice in the back of her mind whispered incessantly: run, run, run...

NINETEEN

LETTA

———

Crack. Just as Letta's eyes flew open to the sound, a large *boom* emanated from just outside. She scrambled out of bed in terror and looked up to see smoke trailing up from the meadow outside her window, obscuring the first purple streaks of dawn that had begun to tickle the sky above the trees that surrounded the castle.

Letta's heartbeat quickened as she wiped the dewy windows with her hand. Below she saw two men in the meadow with arrows pointed toward the heavens, tiny sticks tied to them, and… Were the arrows on *fire*?

Simultaneously, the men released the arrows, and she could only watch as the fire reached the attached sticks that flew up, resulting in another *boom*, with smoke and embers flying everywhere into the sky above the castle. The Queen, after that first dinner, had instructed her not to wander outside of the castle in the dark hours because of the dangers present. Was this the sort of threat she had been talking about?

With her heart pounding, she ran to the door to escape, flinging it open only to be met by the Queen and several other women who stood in the doorway. They smiled eagerly at her, the largest number of people she'd seen outside of dinnertime since before her journey here.

"There's fire in the sky!" Letta exclaimed frantically, pointing to the window.

Queen Davena's smile only grew wider and she nodded. "Do you like it?"

Letta's brows furrowed, surprised by the woman's calm demeanor. "What do you mean?"

Her soon-to-be mother-in-law gently grasped her by the elbow and walked her back to the window. "It is Apasian custom to have our firemasters awaken the bride on her wedding day. It is quite a lovely sight to wake up to, is it not?"

"It's... not... an attack?"

"Heavens, no," the woman chuckled, motioning to the view. Now that Letta knew it was done with the Queen's blessing, she took the chance to observe the sight. It *was* quite remarkable, now that she looked at it. She watched in awe as the small orange embers flared up to light the dark violet sky, shooting higher than the castle *and* the trees, with thin lines of smoke emanating from them. She had never seen anything like it in Padaure and couldn't help but wonder what other surprises were in store for her today.

The other ladies had waltzed over to the windows as well, delighted at the sight, and watched until the men ceased to fire their arrows. The orange rays of a rising sun had just started to seep in from behind the trees that surrounded the castle grounds.

"Alright, ladies, the spectacle is over," the Queen announced, turning to the rest with a beaming face. "Let's get our bride ready for her day."

The air in the room was filled with so many sickeningly sweet perfumes and powders that Letta wasn't sure if she would ever be able to breathe normally again. Although the castle itself seemed to be isolated from the capital, it felt as if all of Apasia's citizens filled the halls, and half of them were beautifying Letta for her wedding day.

One lady twirled and twisted and tied her hair into an intricate braided bun as another three sewed and tightened her dress around the shoulders, bust, and waist. It was quite elegant, she had to admit, in a soft white fabric with small, complex green tulip designs stitched into the hem. The design was traditionally used in the royal family for weddings and special occasions, she had been told. Yet another two women powdered her face, covering her eyelids in a light green powder and painting a rosy color on her cheeks to "give more life" to her naturally pale face.

Hours dragged on, with high-pitched compliments of "the Prince is such a lucky man!" and "what beautiful thick hair!" and "the loveliest eyes in Apasia!" flooding her ears. Perhaps she would have appreciated them individually any other time, but it just seemed like shallow flattery to her, words said by strangers to appeal to their future Princess.

The thought shook her as she came to that realization. She would be Princess, and one day Queen of Apasia, a country in which she had spent only a few weeks' time, married to a man she currently saw only briefly at dinner times. He'd been soft-spoken, only animated in the one moment they had shared alone.

And her? She was still just Letta, a Duke's daughter from a foreign country who spent her days with her nose in books, too awkward to even try to compare to the regal presence of the current Queen, who could silence a room simply by the confident gait with which she entered. Would she ever be good enough? Was she really ready for what came, whenever it *would* come?

The entire day was just a replication of what her time here had felt like—a blur, a girl lost in her own thoughts as people and life spun around her, only the rare moment spent with a familiar face. Men and women alike rushed by, scrutinizing her appearance, arguing over how to perfect it for the pleasure of the Prince and all who would come to the ceremony that night. Letta hoped she could at least make her family proud and look the part for their sakes as well, so they would know they'd made the right decision in marrying her off here.

It was all happening so quickly that when she found herself walking down the aisle that evening, led by King Dobrilo, she wasn't quite sure how she'd gotten there. The eyes of many nobles from the area—as well as the faces of her Padaurean family and some of her father's friends—were all on her, with reactions varying from tiny smiles to teary beams. She prayed she wouldn't trip on the dress that trailed behind her as she passed what must have been at least two hundred people. Her gaze met the eyes of her sister, which shone with tears that welled up in them, and Letta couldn't tell whether they were of prideful joy for a lovely ceremony or nostalgic sorrow for a sister who moved away. Perhaps it was both.

The room was elaborately decorated with white roses and red-and-purple tulips lining her path in the dark-green carpet and matching the bouquet in her hand. Tall, thick candles surrounded the room under the green banners of the deer sigil on the walls, adding a nice, soft glow to the room underneath the candles in the chandelier above and filling the room with light while illuminating the faces around them.

She finally found her Prince in front of her, his porcelain face and sharp cheekbones looking almost delicate in the golden light. His sky-blue eyes looked as if they had also been lost in thought, and he seemed almost surprised to see his bride suddenly in front of him.

He looked down for a brief moment as he took a deep breath. He ran his fingers through his neatly combed black hair, even though she hadn't noticed any part of it to be out of place, before looking back at his father.

Standing by the minister, the King's voice boomed as he gave some flowery speech about blessing the union that would become of two beautiful noble youths from two wonderful kingdoms tonight. The words were nice, she was sure, but she had a hard time getting out of her own head enough to listen to them.

Letta's eyes remained on her Prince, speculating about what the rest of their lives would be like. From their limited interactions, she could sense that he was intelligent, and a bit like her—perhaps her father had had the same feeling—but she also felt like there was something more, something deeper to him. She wondered what it was. What had everyone been so hush-hush about in her time here thus far? What secrets were they hiding? She resolved to find out. At the very least, he *seemed* interesting enough that perhaps royal life wouldn't be as boring as she'd dreaded it to be, if she could only see him more often.

She returned to reality when the Prince's warm hands had taken hers, and he repeated the vows of the minster, promising to take care of her and work with her for both the family they would have and the kingdom they would rule.

She doubted he'd written the words himself. He seemed to have memorized phrases like "We will establish a lovely union, for the home, for the kingdom, and for the Continent itself." Yet the way he looked into her eyes convinced her that he meant it still.

As her turn came, she mindlessly repeated the vows as well, and before she knew it, they were turning to face the audience behind them and holding hands as everyone clapped for the newlywed couple. Letta looked back into the crowd to see her sister's tear-streaked, adoring smile. Her mother seemed on the verge of tears herself, and her father wore a stern pride in the beam on his face.

After what felt like ages of nobles and people of the court coming up to the royal table to congratulate her and her husband for their marriage, Letta took a moment to sink back into her chair. Apasians and Padaureans alike enjoyed dancing, but the highest-ranked royals were expected to maintain their seats at the table in front of the hall for the most part, to her relief. So she felt right at home as she sat beside her new mother-in-law, surveying the room.

She noticed her new husband had ducked out, along with the King and his brother, as soon as they had scarfed down their meals and finished with their greetings. Not that she should have been surprised, given their general absences even at night, but she was still a bit disappointed. When she tried to inquire about it, the Queen dismissed her concerns with a remark about the men in the noble family "going off to celebrate in a small family tradition."

"What sort of tradition might that be?"

Davena shrugged, picking at a piece of dessert that had been served to them on small plates. "It is something that the men tend to keep to themselves. I would not be the one to ask."

Nodding, Letta opened her mouth to try to ask more before her sister walked up to the table, curtsying to the Queen and then to her. Letta tried not to laugh to herself. Less than a month ago, her sister had been talking her ear off and jumping on her bed, and here she was now with royal pleasantries thrown between the two of them. She did seem a bit more grown-up in some strange way. Perhaps it was the cosmetics or the lighting.

Nevertheless, the new Princess was happy to get a glimpse of the familiar, gleeful character of her sister, as she leaned in to whisper, "I've made it halfway through that book of yours, Letta."

"Oh?" Letta's eyebrows raised, surprised that she had already made it so far.

"I can see why you enjoy it—even though it could use a bit more romance," her sister teased.

"Of course, *you'd* think that," Letta poked back, betraying a smile. "I hope you enjoy the rest of it. Write me what you think once you do finish it."

Atora grinned. "I cannot wait," she promised. As the bards started playing one of her favorite songs, she looked back at her sister, who gave her a nod to say *go ahead*. Leaning over the table, the younger sister kissed her on the cheek and said, "Best of luck with everything. I can't wait to hear more about your new husband!"

It was a nice exchange, and Letta was happy to see the girl go off to light up the room, dancing with other noblemen for the first time as an eligible young woman, now that the older sister had been married off.

"Not a dancer?" the Queen asked her.

Letta shook her head.

"I'm afraid I must ask where your sister gets that from," she continued with a smile.

The Princess laughed. "My mother, for sure. My father and I tend to prefer the quiet."

"Mhm. I don't blame you," her mother-in-law said. "My son is the same way." She took a deep breath and looked back at the girl. "I must say, the more I learn about you, the happier I am that you are joined to him. You seem to match each other very well."

"We do?" Letta asked, trying to hide that she was dying to learn more about her absentee husband. "I wish I could learn that from seeing it with my own eyes," she said wistfully.

Queen Davena nodded, leaning in to whisper, "If you would like, I can continue to entertain the guests here while you get away. I imagine time with your new husband would be something you might like." She winked, and it took Letta a second to put together what she was implying.

"Oh!" she said, heat rising in her cheeks, surprised at the Queen's casual attitude with what her parents had considered too taboo to seriously bring up with her. "Sure, yes. I mean, only if he'd want—"

The Queen laughed again. "My son is many things, but blind is not one of them." She laid a friendly hand on Letta's upper arm. "I'll send for the servants to fetch him and bring him to you."

Letta nodded nervously, taking a deep breath and waving goodbye to her family as she let one of the servants lead her away to her new chambers.

The entry to their chambers was quite exquisite. The walls were covered in those same intricate walnut carvings, complemented by brown-toned tapestries with a grand chandelier above a bright red carpet in the entry room. The hues seemed muted in contrast to the flashes of color she had seen from the dress of the nobles who had peppered the floor in the main hall for the dancing, but it was a quieter, warmer atmosphere, far enough away that she had stopped hearing the constant chatter that had so overwhelmed her.

She passed between two spiral columns and then walked up a short couple of steps to enter a room with squared shapes beveled into the walls that held small landscape paintings. The quiet filled her up with a new sort of energy. She would finally be able to spend time with her Prince, in peace.

The floor here was covered by brown-and-white floral carpets, with a couple of chaises covered by white embroidered silk that shone in the light of the more modest chandelier above.

She liked it this way, a seemingly simpler room with tiny, beautiful details to admire. Letta could imagine herself sitting on the chaise in the candlelight, reading books from the royal collection and lying on the bed talking to her husband about them. That really *would* be the life. Wouldn't it?

The Princess walked to the bed, which had two sets of candles on a shelf above it to light up the area. She sat on the soft, white quilt with intricately woven designs of red and purple, matching the colors of the flowers that had surrounded her during their wedding ceremony.

Reminiscing on how lovely the place had looked, she felt sorry that her anxiety and tendency to overthink had prevented her from truly taking in the atmosphere as much as she could have. Fiddling with the fabric on her dress anxiously, she told herself that Merek was due to show up anytime now.

Or was he? Minutes passed by, or what felt like hours. Perhaps it *was* hours. She tried to distract herself by looking around and taking in every single detail, but there were only so many details she could observe, only so many times she could circle around the room and ponder where he was and what was going on. Should she go back to the party? She couldn't. What if he returned to the room to find her absent? Besides, she didn't have the energy to go back and deal with all those people or the questions the Queen might ask.

Stupid traditions, she thought, sighing and wondering how much longer she'd have to wait before he'd come to bed. Or what if he realized he didn't want her after all and that he'd prefer to spend time with his brother? Or even... with a *whore*?

She made herself dizzy with all the intrusive thoughts that buzzed around in her head. Eventually, fatigue took over and she lay down on the left side of her large, new bed. The mattress was soft and welcoming, but it didn't do much to make her feel any less lonely.

This was supposed to be her wedding night—supposedly the happiest night of any maiden's life, when she would consummate her marriage to the Prince and officially become Apasian royalty once and for all. She would finally get to spend more time with him. But just as was the case for the past few weeks, he was nowhere to be found, and she found herself still in her wedding dress, drifting off alone in a disappointing silence with a tear-soaked pillow.

TWENTY

JASPER

———

Tracing the white scars that laced over his unwrapped forearms, Jasper tried yet again to see if he could replicate the feeling Onyx had given him when she'd accidentally brushed up against them a few nights before. Nothing. They remained white, but didn't glow and didn't send the same pulsing energy tingling through them and into his veins as she had.

Was this a side effect of accidental skin-to-skin contact? It couldn't be. He'd probably had some sort of accidental brush with other people like that, whether in grappling or sex, but he was sure he'd remember that sort of feeling if he'd had it before.

And he realized that he had on that first night with Onyx. He'd attributed the strange feeling to just an intimate sensation, and perhaps it was. But the second time he'd ever felt that way had been this accidental brush with her, not in grappling. What about her triggered such an intoxicating response? As he tightly wrapped his forearms in the silk, tying them up past his elbow this time to avoid slipping, he resolved to find out.

The day was a casual and slow one. Jasper had some of his men bring in hay bales from the local stables and paint targets on them for archery practice, stratifying the practices by difficulty, as usual.

"Any soldier who hits to satisfaction on the ground will graduate to shooting from the second-story windows," he instructed, pointing to those windows that faced the targets in the courtyard. "And once you're good on the second story, you may go to the third."

Meanwhile, the more experienced archers kept guard in the castle's archer towers, with the order to practice a bit by aiming at the hay bales they'd placed on the ground there, taking turns running up and down the stairs to the tower and out to the bales to retrieve the arrows. Jasper figured it wouldn't hurt to have them brush up on their skills as well, especially since it was unheard of for people to dare to attack the castle in peacetime. The job could get boring, so they might as well make themselves of some use.

Back in the courtyard, however, he observed Onyx. Nothing seemed out of the ordinary with her. She remained focused on refining her skills as usual. Jasper couldn't help but watch her gracefully pulling the string back over and over as if it were a mindless instinct, those dark eyes narrowing as they fixated on the target, those slender fingers swiftly releasing the arrow to lead to a *thwang*.

To no one's surprise, she had graduated to the third-floor practice within the first hour. Jasper knew she would remain there at the window for the rest of the day, or at least until he ordered her to do something else, but he didn't want to send her to the archers' windows in the castle. He wanted her here, so he could observe her more closely. But there was no reason to have her down on the courtyard-level with him, not without arousing suspicion that something more than professional was going on, so he had to settle for the separation and do his best to focus on the recruits.

Before he knew it, the sun started to sink out of his sight, still illuminating the sky and the city but blocked by the third story of the soldiers' quarters. It was time to call it a day for the men. Most of them had made good progress, and only a couple of them hadn't made it past the second story.

As he dismissed the soldiers, his glance naturally fell on Onyx. He watched her pull out the last of the arrows she'd fired. Her eyes flitted over to him, and for a split second their gazes met. Jasper's heart skipped a beat and he looked away quickly, crossing his arms and pretending to take an interest in the post-training boys' talk. When he glanced back over, she was gone.

Back in his room, he obsessively unwrapped his forearms again. Still nothing, to his chagrin. He re-wrapped them, pacing back and forth in his room. *You're overthinking again. Maybe it's time to see if it's not too late to join the men for drinks and get your mind off it.*

Walking out of the castle, he stopped by the Sergeants' doors in the soldiers' quarters. Osbert's door was unlocked, leading to an empty room, and the same went for Tarren. Sighing, he decided to walk out to the courtyard and find his way there himself. They were probably already at the Maiden's Mug, as usual.

Darkness fell over the courtyard, as the sun had just sunk below the horizon. Jasper caught a door opening out of the corner of his eye. Turning to see Onyx in a black cloak, peeking her head out, he hid behind a pillar and watched her from the shadows. It seemed she hadn't noticed him. Pulling up the hood of her cloak over her head, she concealed her braid and much of her face, rushing out of the quarters.

Jasper followed her, trying to keep a safe distance and an eye on her although it was already getting difficult with shadows seeping into the corners and onto the streets. She turned off the cobblestone roads into the nearby field, circling the grassy areas around the castle to enter the forest a few hundred feet behind it.

The trees seemed to pass on by, and he tried to keep up, frustrated at how she seemed so able to move so quickly and soundlessly with little effort.

Eventually, he found himself at the base of a small mountain, watching from behind a conifer as she nimbly scaled a scree that grew steeper and steeper. The last ten feet of her ascent turned into a vertical wall.

"For a Royal Guard, you aren't as silent as you think you are. You might as well join me here," she said, as she mantled herself into the ledge at the top.

Surprised, he hesitated for a moment before deciding to join her, trying not to trip on the pebbles that covered the slab of rock. He wasn't sure how, but he made it up to her ledge, although not nearly as quickly as she had managed it. The climb looked so easy when she did it. After all, her strength was a lot more concentrated in that lithe body, and she had less weight to pull up.

As he dragged his body over the ledge, he found a small cave—just large enough to provide shelter and small enough to see the end of it, even in the limited moonlight. He sat down, leaning against the rocky wall and watching her with a sense of anxiety. She sat right at the ledge with her legs crossed before turning to face him.

"You really need to work on your climbing, Lieutenant," she chaffed. "It's rather sloppy."

Easy for her to say. We don't need to train for that. He rolled his eyes and caught his breath, looking out at the forest sixty feet below them and then back at her.

"So what would be your motive for following me?" Onyx continued. "Bored? Curious? Or just the slightest bit lonely?"

"What are you doing here?" he asked, ignoring her snide comments.

She laughed, turning her head to look out. "I like the view."

He followed her gaze and took a moment to absorb the view of the forest blanketed in darkness that spread out vastly in the horizon, the treetops illuminated only by the patches of moonlight that escaped from behind every other cloud.

"We both know what I mean. You show up and sleep with me—"

"Something you didn't seem to mind. *You* invited me inside, if I recall correctly," she smirked.

"But then you disappear for weeks. Now you come back and try to join the Royal Guard—"

"I didn't *try* to join. I *did* join, at the King's request," she interrupted again.

Jasper ignored her comment. He was getting more worked up. "Then you go attacking my brother and disappearing at night, and then doing some weird... I don't know... witch-craft, whatever the hell it is... to my scars." The sly smile disappeared from her face, along with its color. "Who are you *really*, and what are you doing in Padaure?"

She took a deep breath. "You're by far the smartest one around here. I figured you'd start asking questions at some point." Onyx readjusted her seating, scooting closer to him and leaning in. "But if this conversation leaves this spot, I have a dulling knife that I haven't used in a while."

He tried to ignore the threat, knowing he *could* overtake her, but still, he felt uneasy after seeing what she was capable of in training. He wondered what else she excelled at. The Lieutenant found it in himself to look her directly in the eyes. "You don't scare me."

A half-smirk returned to her face. "If that was true, you wouldn't have followed me here."

He swallowed, his guts tightening. Letting out an exasperated breath, he motioned with his hand for her to continue with her explanation.

"First of all, he still has his *royal jewels,* so he's in much better condition than others who have tried." Jasper tried not to wince or think too deeply about what she was suggesting. "And you know that *prick* isn't really your brother."

His brows furrowed. "What does that have to do with—?"

"We know each other from before that night, though we didn't seem to recognize one another at first." Noting his confusion, she shuffled closer, holding out her hand for him to take. Gingerly, he complied. Her hand was cold and callused, and she began to roll back his sleeves with her other one. The white energy gently returned as a pleasant heat seeping in and lighting up the laceration scars.

Jasper started, that familiar feeling of warmth filling him. "What are you—?"

"Do you remember where you got these from?" Onyx whispered softly, cutting him off with an intense stare.

Hesitating at first, the Lieutenant looked back at those scars that had begun to glow with that same pulsating heat that seemed to move in sync with his heartbeats. He tried to block out the memories of the excruciating burning sensation, the shadow that had covered the village before the monster landed on a few cottages. The roofs that had erupted in purple flames and the screams that accompanied them started resurfacing. Eventually, he took a breath and replied, "I try not to."

She let him go and turned around, moving her long, thick braid to the front and removing her cloak. She rolled down the top part of her clothing to expose her upper back. He wondered what she was doing before realizing she was covered in the same types of scars that painted his forearms.

Lifting his hand, he softly traced his fingers on the warm skin of her upper back, noticing her shiver at the first touch. He flinched as he watched her laceration scars glow as well. He couldn't help but wonder how much he'd had to drink that night, to spend it with her and not notice this. Had he even taken *everything* off?

Rolling up her clothing, Onyx covered herself back up and moved by his side, also leaning against the rocky wall. Reaching into the folds of her cloak, she brandished a small, slightly translucent stone that shone a light purple in the sliver of moonlight that hit it. She held it out in the palm of her hand and motioned for him to touch it as well. Unsure of what exactly was going on, he lightly brushed it with his fingertips.

Suddenly, he was taken back to that familiar little village in the mountains. In daylight now, they saw people strolling down the paths lined with the trees that stood over their heads as they happily greeted one another. There were no beggars, no noblemen, only simply dressed villagers selling food or flowers, content as they watched their children running down the streets laughing.

The scene morphed again, and he saw two men sitting back at a table drinking and telling stories as their wives chatted and cooked in the nearby kitchen, from what he could hear. The men looked over adoringly, and Jasper followed their gazes to find what must have been their children. They couldn't have been older than three or four at this point, playing with a petite blonde who appeared to be in her twenties.

There was a little girl, who he could instantly tell was Onyx with slightly lighter honey-brown hair, braided with small purple lilacs, and the same dark eyes. The other two were twin boys with wavy dark hair and olive skin. The only difference seemed to lay in their eyes. One of the boys' was a green so brilliant they almost seemed to glow, and the other had... hazel. Just like Jasper's.

Just as the realization took over, the scene changed again to one he tried to forget to this day. The heart of the village lay under a dark sky, as if a thunderstorm were about to happen. Violet flames surrounded them as did the screams of the locals who had either been set afire or trapped in their collapsing homes.

A large, winged creature, its chest alone twice the size of any house around, with scales so silver they appeared to be glowing among the flames, landed on the ground. As it stood up taller, Jasper could see the balaur more clearly, its seven necks so long that he couldn't see all of the heads that reached into the alleys.

But one of the heads looked straight ahead at him. Its eyes glowed a bright lavender and its mouthful of jagged teeth were bared, its spit shining in the reflection of the flames and solidifying as it fell off of the monster's black, forked tongue. A ball of purple energy began to emanate in its mouth as it faced him.

He tried to pull his brother, who faced the monster and froze out of fear, with him behind the wall. Just before the flames hit, he was taken back to that quiet mountaintop, left looking at his forearms, a new energy turning his laceration scars into a bright, burning purple as his vision turned black.

When Jasper regained consciousness, he found his head resting in someone's lap with fingers running idly through his hair, soothing him the same way his mother had, years and years ago. But she was gone now. Jolting himself up, he scrambled back to find Onyx sitting there in the same cave with him, a concerned look on her face as he tried to reorient himself, distressed from whatever she'd just cast on him.

"C-Citrina?" he asked, remembering her name now.

She nodded soberly.

"What just happened?" Jasper asked, rubbing his temples, still shaken up from the visions.

"With the stone?"

"The stone, the scars, everything."

Onyx—no—Citrina hesitated for a moment. "Have you ever had this kind of thing happen before? Strange energies, powers from crystals, anything of the sort?"

He shook his head. "No, never thought there was such a thing."

She sighed, staring blankly at the ground. "They say those who survive a balaur's burns develop unseen… abilities…" Citrina looked back up at him. "At the very least, that was the case for me. I can transfer energies from crystals and use that for the desired effect, like I did to enhance your memories. Over the years, I experimented with it and collected different stones.

"I'm sorry, though, I didn't think the memory would get that intense for you. Usually, I don't have people passing out on me from that."

"Have you used these on me before?"

She laughed. "I've tried perhaps once or twice."

"What about the whole—" He motioned to his forearms, which were only faintly glowing now.

He was disappointed when she shook her head. "I'm sorry. While I know other people who survived the *attack*, you're the first other person I've met who survived the burns. I can't say I have the faintest idea why that happens."

"There are others?"

Citrina nodded. "My parents, just like yours, died that night, but a family friend found me and fled, raising me and moving from place to place.

"Until recently, we assumed you and your brother—your *real* brother, that is—along with the rest of the village, were dead. The moment I saw your scars, I knew I was at least partially wrong."

Jasper nodded, his twin brother's young face flashing into his mind for a moment. He wasn't quite sure what to say—or rather, which of the million questions in his mind he wanted to ask next. Tracing her features with his line of sight, he took her in. Yes, he faintly recalled that little girl now, her sweet laugh and the beautiful purple lilacs that her mother would lace through her hair.

The adult Citrina stared back at him. He noticed her glance drop to his lips before slowly finding its way back to his eyes; their gazes locked. Just as Jasper found himself leaning in, she broke eye contact and looked back out.

"We should return now," she said, rising to her feet.

Taking a deep breath, he followed her, scaling down the mountain and walking through the forest. The trees looked ominous in their thick coats of shadow, but a strange peace surrounded them, as if they were the only two people left in the world. He found he didn't completely mind the feeling.

"Make me a promise," she whispered, looking at him with pleading eyes, "that you don't tell anyone my true name. Please."

"How come?" He stopped in the darkness, and so did she.

Citrina shook her head. "That's a story for another time. When we're in Padaure, call me Onyx and nothing else, and tell no one about anything that happened between us."

Jasper took her hand in both of his, looking at her intently. "I'm not trying to lose my position, nor do I want to lose my best soldier." She smiled shyly, looking down. With a finger, he pulled her chin up so she'd look at him again. "I promise."

Her smile grew just a little, and she seemed a little less tense as they continued walking. She kept one of her hands clasped with his throughout the forest, letting go only at the first sight of Padaure.

The two of them stopped just by the edge of the forest, and Citrina turned to look at him, He silently stared into her eyes, finding himself reaching up to brush her cheek and leaning in with an overwhelming urge to kiss her.

As if she read his mind, she gave him a halfhearted smile. "Perhaps another time. Goodnight, Jasper."

A shiver ran through his body with the way she said his name, and he could only watch as she pulled the hood back over her head. Her figure retreated into the fields and headed back to the soldiers' quarters. Not entirely sure what he was feeling or what to think, he stood there in the shadows of the trees even after she'd disappeared from his line of sight.

TWENTY-ONE

OTRA

——

Otra followed Vitor through the marketplace, listening to him as he explained the quirks and customs of the Allied Cities of Lebiros. It was fascinating to her, how they consolidated their resources for redistribution to its people, how their culture emphasized giving and kindness, how they didn't believe in monarchs but rather in commonfolk and rich folk sharing power for the better of all. It sounded almost like paradise to her, and she couldn't wait to tell Lumina all about it.

After all, the information from Vitor *did* help her in her scouting mission. In fact, it made her task even easier with someone to guide her through it, whether or not he realized what exactly he was doing. She even found a chink or two in the armor of this society. *If it's so simple to get commonfolk in power, perhaps it would be quite easy to get a person or two from the Phoenix in on the deal as well.*

What she enjoyed almost as much was watching him interact with the others around him. He was magnetic, the kind of man whose smile lit up every corner of any street he walked on. Children loved him, and why wouldn't they? He was a generous soul, buying the odd apple to toss to any slightly undernourished child, who would embrace him gratefully.

She wondered how differently her life would have turned out had someone like him showed her that sort of kindness at all growing up. Lumina was a kind soul, that was for sure, and she had nurtured Otra alongside Citrina. But Vitor acted in kindness without regard for loyalty. The children's admiration for him seemed to be something he didn't even notice, nor did he seem to take note of the women who shot Otra jealous looks as they walked past.

And yet he was spending time with *her*. Besides her secretiveness about her identity and the fact that she was foreign to the place, she didn't see what would entice him to spend so much time with her—to sweep her off her feet, dancing, buying her drinks, holding her without expecting anything more, talking with her for hours on end about life in Lebiros and their traditions. It drove her crazy, trying to figure out what he wanted and doing everything she could to read him but to no avail. She knew he worked as an advisor to the Lebirosi Council, but he talked so openly about the mundaneness of his position that it took a large stretch of the imagination to honestly get the impression that he was hiding anything at all.

"Do you like flowers?" he asked, out of nowhere.

"Flowers?" she asked, confused. No one had ever asked her such a strange question, nor had she ever paid attention enough to any sort of plant to think about whether or not she liked them. "I suppose they are nice."

He stopped by a stand, tossing a coin to the short, balding man who returned a rose. "For you," Vitor said, handing it to her.

Trying not to prick herself from the sparse, tiny thorns, she admired the flower in her hand—a bright, sunset orange, rich in color. She smelled it, taking in the feel of the soft petals tickling her nose and the intoxicatingly delightful scent that accompanied it. "It's lovely," she admitted shyly, not sure whether to mention that no one had ever gotten her one before, especially not without reason. She looked back up at him incredulously. "Why?"

A boyish grin painted his face. "Why not?"

Before she knew it, the sun was setting. She found herself in his arms again as a chord struck, followed by fiddles and harpsichords melodiously accompanying the voices that filled the square, a soft glow coating every little corner. The square seemed a bit brighter. She wasn't sure if that was actually the case, or if being there with Vitor, in his arms, made it feel that way.

Now that she had seen more of him, better understanding his character, at least as far as she knew, she hoped it wasn't some elaborate act. While she had been a pretender among these people, she found that even if she refused to tell him her name, she couldn't fool him about anything either—not only because of his aptitude for catching lies but also under the influence of the sincerity with which he carried himself.

"Otra," she confessed at the end of the song.

"Pardon?" he asked, tilting his head and stopping while the first few notes of the next song played.

"Otra," she repeated. "That's my name. Honest."

He beamed at her, as if satisfied—not in a malicious, soliciting way so much as in an appreciative way. "Otra," he echoed, tracing her face with his eyes and then leaning in for a moment to whisper in her ear, his breath making her shiver. "It fits you. I knew you had to have a beautiful name."

Heat filled her cheeks, and she returned his smile. Letting him lead her into another dance, she felt even lighter on her feet, as if he had just lifted a weight off of her that she hadn't even been aware she was carrying.

The night continued to fly by, and she felt even lighter and lighter, a new sort of fluttery feeling spreading throughout her chest. It was a bit scary. She had never felt something like that before, but it felt *exciting* as well.

She found herself walking back to that same inn with him before lying down on the bed and laughing at some silly joke he'd made. All alone with only their whispers and giggles to fill the silence in the room, they didn't care if they were pissing off the neighbors.

Turning her head, she found his already angled toward her, those large, dark brown eyes softening up as he leaned in. Otra turned the rest of her body toward him as he cupped her cheek in his hand and brought her lips to his, sliding closer until her body completely pressed up against his. He rolled on top of her, pinning her to the bed so she couldn't escape, and she found she liked that. She liked it even more when she slid her hands up his shirt and how his bare skin felt on hers as he slipped everything off...

As the sunlight trickled in through the cracks in the inn's curtains, she slowly opened her eyes to see her dress on the floor. Remembering the night before, she closed her eyes again for a second and smiled. She thought of how invigorating it had felt to have Vitor's eyes taking in all of her, his skin against hers, his lips trailing all over her body...

All over her body? Frantically, she peered at her forearms, noticing that the sleeves she often had on were taken off, exposing her branding. She didn't recall doing that.

"I see you're awake," his voice called monotonously. As she sat up against the head of the bed, she saw a dressed

Vitor leaning against the wall on the other side of the room with his arms and ankles crossed, eyes trained on her as if he'd watched her all this time. She opened her mouth to speak, but he interrupted her. "You're endlessly full of secrets, aren't you?"

Otra covered her bare chest with the blanket while she reached for her dress, turning her forearms to herself even though she knew it was futile. There was no way he hadn't seen them by now. "I doubt I'm the only one," she accused, attempting a nonchalant tone as she slipped back into her dress.

He scoffed. "I've been nothing but honest with you."

"As if there's nothing you're hiding from me."

"Not at all, actually," Vitor argued, rubbing one of his temples and looking away toward the window. "I can't believe I was so stupid. Of course, you'd be here to use me. That's probably why you asked so many questions."

Her heart felt like it dropped out of her chest. She stood up. "Vitor—"

"Save it." Her lover's voice was bitter.

"I won't," she argued, walking to him. "It's not at all what you think it is."

Glaring at her, he replied, "Really? Because it seems a lot to me like you're a Phoenix." He jutted his chin toward her forearm. "Everything I'd heard about your... people... I'd dismissed as a myth, like everyone else." He lowered his voice, as if trying to disguise the rage he felt, a look of disgust on his face. "But it's true. So what are you? An assassin here to get information out of me then kill me?"

Otra was silent for a moment. Technically, she'd used that technique before. She shook her head, but he didn't seem convinced.

"You know, you're *exactly* the kind of person I'm supposed to watch out for, to report as a threat to the Allied Cities."

Otra laid a gentle hand on his arm. "And have you?"

He stiffened, breaking eye contact and taking in a breath. He looked down for a moment before shaking his head a little bit. "Not yet."

A small wave of relief washed over her and she let out a breath, her hand sliding off.

"Don't think that I won't," he warned, looking back to her.

"Oh, I fully believe you can," she replied.

"And yet you're calm."

She let out a short laugh under her breath. "The farthest from it. I'm more conflicted than anything else."

"Is this *conflict* the only thing preventing you from killing me?"

Turning, she froze upon looking back into those dark eyes. "Why do you think I avoided you so much at first?"

"I thought you were playing games, that you *wanted* me to chase you."

She paused to think for a moment. Now that he said it, she realized a part of her *had* wanted him to pursue her, even aside from his position in the city. A part of her wanted *him* in general, and she had succumbed to that part. "Because I didn't want *this* to happen."

"What is *this*, exactly?"

Throwing up her hands in the air, Otra paced through the room. "I don't know! All I know is that I *always* kill men before they get the chance to…" She gestured vaguely.

"Not *always*," he corrected her.

She stopped, her eyes meeting his again. "Not anymore."

Vitor raised his brows, his jaw dropping a bit as he searched her eyes. It seemed he hadn't expected that answer. "I'm… I'm the f—"

"The first, yes," she admitted, looking at her feet and trying to ignore the suffocating silence that followed.

He decided to break it with a deep breath, running his fingers through his curly locks. "So what were you planning to do with me… after… you know…"

"I don't know, Vitor." She exhaled, sitting on the edge of the bed and rubbing her temples. "I just… let it happen. I don't know what it is about you. I just feel like when you're around, I've escaped from everything and can just… enjoy myself, in the moment. I forget about everything else when I'm with you."

"So you're *not* planning to kill me?"

Otra found it in her to look back up at him. "Not unless you're planning to kill *me*."

She felt as though he was looking into her, searching for a lie, and this time, he would be disappointed. For the first time, she was exposing herself—*all* of herself—to someone outside of the Phoenix. She was possibly committing treason, and though her chest tightened in anticipation of what he might say, she also felt… liberated?

Their eyes locked, and she wanted to look away but couldn't. What *was* she going to do now? Lumina would want her to tie up this loose end that would confirm the Phoenix's existence to the public, the one suitor of hers to know her true name, who she really was. But she couldn't bring herself to even reach for her knife. It seemed that neither of them knew what to do with the other.

After a long silence, his eyes lit up. "What if I could give you the gift of nothing to escape from?"

Furrowing her eyebrows, she wasn't sure if he had gone mad. "What do you mean, nothing to escape from?"

He walked up to her, taking her hands in his. "What if you join me here? In Lebiros. You could live a different life without having to court and kill and sneak around."

The thought enticed her. While she was excellent at what she did—scouting, seducing, and killing, putting to justice loose ends and abusers—she wondered what it would be like if she wasn't tied to the Phoenix, if she were left to her own devices. She recalled that little kid Vitor had tossed an apple to in the market square. Perhaps it wasn't too late to change her path, to be like that child. Maybe to even have one of her own, roaming the streets careless and happy and free.

"No one to report to, no one to listen to but ourselves," she whispered, glancing between their intertwined hands and his face, a beautiful golden tone in the rays of the late dawn.

Vitor nodded eagerly. Leaning over, he gave her a soft, slow kiss on her knuckles. "I would take care of you. Make sure no one hurts you. You'd never have to worry about protecting yourself again."

"Vitor," she whispered, and his eyes looked at her hopefully. "I would love that."

A smile grew on his face. "So it's settled then?"

She looked down at her forearms, at the branding, the bird that had been etched into her skin years ago, and the forty-four tallies she had put on herself. Could she really leave? It would mean putting a target on her back among people who lived a mundane life. It would mean letting the corrupt men of the world run around touching little girls and stealing money from their citizens, allowing the various Kings and royals to get away with rejecting people like her in their greatest time of need. It would mean hurting and abandoning Lumina, Citrina, and the rest of the group that had raised her, that had saved her from a life of actual prostitution. And that was not who she was, even putting aside their death penalty for treason.

Her eyes watered, and she blinked, looking down and hoping he wouldn't notice. But of course, he would. They were too close for him not to see everything.

With that, she shook her head, a tear trailing down her cheek. "I can't."

It broke her heart to say, especially when paired with glancing up and watching how his eyes fell. That small part of her, along with her feelings for him, had grown without her wanting to admit it. It screamed at her to take it back, to leave her life behind to be with him. But it wasn't the right thing to do. What would she do with herself if she had to live with betraying the only family she'd known?

Vitor's face fell, and he nodded solemnly. "I understand."

"I'm sorry," she whispered, trying to stop her voice from shaking. "You haven't the slightest idea how difficult it is for me to say it."

He leaned over and gave her a long, lingering kiss on the forehead, pulling her into one last embrace. He held her as if it was the last time he ever would. It probably would be.

"Just get out, as soon as you can," he warned, and she could only watch as he walked out of the room, away from her, not bothering to look back.

TWENTY-TWO

ANGHEL

With crossed arms, Anghel leaned against the stone frame of the soldiers' court entryway, waiting for his friends to finish their training before their routine drinks. Among the dust clouds that billowed, he observed them in action, some grappling and some practicing their sword-fighting with short wooden poles. Part of him wished he was there, getting in on the action. It'd be more interesting than the pointless politics he was half-subject to in the castle.

He watched Jasper look up to see the sun out of sight, nodding to himself and giving the soldiers his usual clear, crisp command that training was over for the day. The Lieutenant nodded and patted the occasional recruit, giving them advice on how to better their form mixed with praise.

His brother had an admirable talent, not only in just about any form of combat imaginable but also in elevating others with the right mix of criticism and encouragement. He made a mental note to remind his father what a good job Jasper was doing as Lieutenant.

As the others departed upon their dismissal, the Prince's attention shifted to Onyx, who was helping Jasper pick up the equipment that some of the soldiers had left strewn about.

His gaze was trained on the woman as her eyes met with the Lieutenant's for a second too long, and he watched how her cheeks flushed pink for a moment. He looked over at Jasper, whose eyes had immediately dropped down. The Lieutenant seemed to have a newfound interest in the tiny details on the pole in his hands.

The two continued to clean everything up, and Anghel followed the soldiers into the halls to not seem too suspicious. While his brother wasn't as focused on getting women into bed as Anghel himself was, he was still fine around them. Perhaps to anyone else his dynamic with Onyx might have seemed friendly, but the Prince knew the Lieutenant better than that.

Continuing to keep his eye on the two from a small, curved window in the hall, he saw her hand the equipment to Jasper and start talking to him. While he was too far away to hear what they were saying, he could see her attention fixated on Jasper, as if she were hanging on to every word that came out of his mouth. And Jasper reciprocated it, their eyes again meeting for a bit too long before she looked down and broke the eye contact, running her hand through her hair before looking back up at her Lieutenant.

His brother nodded and kept talking, placing a hand on her arm, and she smiled. It was probably the first time Anghel had seen Onyx genuinely smile. It was a radiant one, the sort that took the Prince by surprise, as it was a stark difference from the serious, no-nonsense version of her that he was used to seeing. As she nodded, the two parted ways, his brother's touch lingering just enough that Anghel almost missed it, but just as he was about to tell himself he'd imagined it, he caught Jasper glancing back at the woman when her back was turned.

"Hey, Prince-y boy, you joinin' us for drinks t'night?" He turned to see his redheaded friend Osbert with a couple of other soldiers.

"I'll join you at the Maiden's Mug in a bit." Anghel smiled. The men nodded and walked out of the hall, their chattering fading away in the late afternoon sun. Anghel walked toward Onyx's chambers in the halls of the soldiers' quarters. With a wince, he recalled the last time he had followed her and how that had ended. It was still strange to him. He was used to women finding him attractive, or at least enticing, but never unwelcome or threatening. Besides, there wouldn't be consequences should anything happen between them. After all, he was no soldier.

He had to be thankful, however. Ladies seemed to find his bruises from that encounter manly, to his advantage—perhaps because he had failed to mention that a woman had given them to him.

But this time was different. He wasn't here for her body. The subtle mannerisms he witnessed when the two thought they were alone clarified everything—why she didn't want him and why she reacted so violently. While he preferred more casual clothing in his spare time, it was still distinct from that of the other soldiers', or so he had thought. Perhaps a chat could further clear things up.

Hesitantly, he knocked on the door. As it opened, Onyx peered out of the crack before slamming it in his face.

Anghel sighed, knocking again. This time, she took longer to open it, making sure to put her hand on the knife sheathed in her thigh strap and keeping that within his line of vision.

"What do you want, Your Highness?" Her voice was even, but its undertones were cold and biting. He couldn't blame her. They had gotten an unfortunate introduction, and he could understand why she'd wish to avoid him.

Raising his hands to show that he meant no harm, he chuckled. "I am not here to have you."

Her eyes narrowed, looking him up and down suspiciously. "What brings you here then, sir?"

He found her confusion amusing, and despite her nonverbal threat, he found himself grinning. He rested his forearm on the doorframe, leaning over her just slightly. "I think I know why you refused me."

Onyx lifted an eyebrow, but her hands didn't drop. "Yes? I believe that was evident... no involvement—"

"I am not a soldier," he cut off, trying not to smile as he shrugged, "so the consequences would be little, if any."

"Perhaps I'm not interested and think it'd be an awful idea regardless," she replied smoothly, crossing her arms.

"Or perhaps someone else has caught your attention—perhaps a certain... *Lieutenant*?"

She leaned out into the hallway, looking in both directions frantically before stepping back with a hollow laugh. "Nice joke. Are you *trying* to get me killed?"

A reaction! It seemed he had been right all along. "Am I correct in my assumption?" he continued, not even trying to hide his playful smirk.

"Quite the contrary, really. I just don't want you spreading lies that might put me in a bad place for no reason." She sighed, smoothing out her sleeves. "Why would I risk my life for a night with anyone here?" She must have observed the doubt on his face because she continued, "While I'm sure you are all *lovely* men, I swore an oath as a loyal soldier to your father. Do you recall that?" Looking down, he almost missed her quiet muttering but couldn't make out what she said.

"Sure," he replied.

"It's the truth," she insisted, confidently staring into his eyes with a serious intensity. The Prince wasn't sure what to say. What had he been thinking? Of course, she wouldn't admit to it… but perhaps he had other ways of figuring out the truth.

"I will believe you," he replied after a short silence, "if you meet me outside of my brother's room in an hour."

She looked confused but narrowed her eyes. "How would I even know where that is?"

Anghel had his doubts, but he couldn't deny she was a decent liar. "In the castle, up the main staircase by the court-yard, fifth door to your right."

Onyx seemed to think about it for a few seconds, before replying, "Wouldn't that be inappropriate for a common soldier to set foot in the castle while off duty? Why should I go?"

He leaned in. "It's an order from your Prince, which over-rides convention. Unless Jasper didn't teach you that part."

Her eyes narrowed again warily, as if she was on the edge of a biting retort, but she held her tongue. Anghel knew he was pushing it, as he often did whenever he pulled the royalty card on Jasper, but he didn't care. His curiosity had gotten the better of him.

She took a deep breath, looking down as if to collect her-self for a moment, and then met his eyes again with a new blankness. "I'll see you then, Your Highness."

Satisfied, Anghel patted her on the shoulder before nod-ding and walking away. He pretended not to hear the door close behind him just a *little* too harshly and laughed quietly to himself. He could hardly wait.

As the Prince walked over with his arm around a woman, he found Onyx waiting outside of Jasper's chambers as ordered, and just as punctual as the Lieutenant himself was. Leaning against the wall, her arms remained crossed even as she noticed the two of them, glancing from head to toe and back up as if sizing up the unfamiliar woman.

Anghel made the effort to introduce them. "Onyx, this is Eva, an old... *friend*... of mine with whom I'm well-acquainted."

Onyx didn't move, and her icy gaze didn't soften. "No thank you, I'm not interested in *acquainting* myself with her the way you have."

"Don't worry. That's not at all my intention," Anghel said, lifting a hand to reassure her. "All I want is the truth."

She took a deep, impatient breath. "You're wasting your time here, as well as mine."

"Am I?"

"You are. I don't think I want to know why you invited me here, or why you decided to bring along a, no offense, whore."

"None taken, miss," Eva said with a placated smile, idly playing with her necklace.

Anghel smirked, taking his arm from around her. Reaching into his pocket, he pulled out a bag of coins to show Eva. The woman nodded, and he put the money back into his pocket before knocking confidently on the door three times. He ignored whatever look Onyx was shooting his way.

Jasper opened the door, seeing the three of them together, and his brows furrowed. Jutting out his chin toward Eva, he asked, "Who's this?"

"My dear brother," Anghel started, failing to hide his grin. "May we come in?"

His brother's expression didn't change, and he was silent for a moment before giving a tired sigh. "What's going on?"

"Well, you see, I had a few suspicions, especially regarding our friend Onyx. But as women do, she denies it, so I was wondering if you could do us both a favor and help… disprove… this suspicion."

Eva walked up to Jasper, sensually moving her hands over his shirt and starting to go under. He tensed up, stepping back with a look of surprise on his face. He glanced over at Onyx and then back to the prostitute, so quickly, that Anghel almost missed it.

"What are you doing?" Jasper asked, gently pushing away the woman.

"A favor," Anghel replied with eyes trained on Onyx, but to his disappointment, he found a bored expression on her face as she leaned against the wall with her arms still crossed. She glanced over at the Prince, as if to say *this is what you called me here for?* He stepped over to the soldier, whispering, "You're not the slightest bit… jealous?"

"As I told you," she said, her voice even and her eyes meeting his confidently, "this is a waste of time. Besides, it seems you're the tempted one." Smirking, she motioned downward with her chin. "Have fun."

Anghel glanced down and felt his cheeks get hot. Looking back up, he saw that Jasper stared after her as she slipped out of their field of vision. Eva had snuck another hand on Jasper's arm, but the Lieutenant wasn't having it, swatting her away while looking after his soldier.

"*Get out,*" the Lieutenant growled, turning to the Prince. His voice was more biting than Anghel had ever heard it before, "*both* of you."

TWENTY-THREE

CITRINA

When Citrina returned to her chambers, she slammed the door, the feeling of nausea growing stronger by the minute. Crouching down over a bucket she'd grabbed on the way, she felt a burning feeling coming up her throat. Something about Padaure seemed to make her sick. Ever since they had taken her in, she'd grown increasingly nauseated at random moments, almost as if her body was trying to warn her about something, though she did her best to hide it from the others.

She spat the rest of the bile in the bucket and lay down in her bed. A wave of fatigue washed over her, and she closed her eyes, breathing slowly and trying not to think about Jasper and the scene she'd just witnessed.

While she was wondering why it had triggered such a strong reaction in her, she realized the admiration she had for her Lieutenant might have been more than professional. Perhaps it was also more apparent than she'd realized if the Prince had caught on to it before she did. Placing a hand over her forehead, she took a few deep breaths, hoping she had at least done a decent job of dissuading him.

Just as she began to drift off, she felt a piercing sensation in her lower abdomen. She grabbed her knife and rushed to sit up, but no one was there. She got dizzy from jumping up too quickly. Pulling up her clothing, she saw no marks on her stomach. Where did that pain come from? She hadn't felt anything like it, even when she did bleed. Something was off, that was for sure. Maybe another modified human was here besides her and Jasper, messing with her. Or maybe that was his power all along?

Searching the room, she found no sign that anything or anyone but her had been there, nor, now that she thought about it, had she heard anything. Was she losing her mind? No, she was probably tired and needed rest. The night was still young, and she wasn't promoted to watch duty yet. She'd have the time for some extra sleep.

After drawing the curtains, she slowly stripped down and dressed for bed, hoping she'd feel better by the time she woke up, whenever that would be. She hadn't been in such a condition since the last time she bled two months ago.

Wait, I haven't bled in two months. She'd been so preoccupied with Jasper and her training that she hadn't even stopped to consider that she'd been dry for longer than usual.

Looking down at her naked body, she saw her stomach was less toned than usual, and she felt the blood drain out of her face. Could she have put on weight? That wouldn't make sense. She hadn't had much of an appetite lately, and she had been training throughout her days here. Her hands softly caressed the area curiously, as she hadn't seen anything like that before, nor did she want to think about what that might mean.

Just breathe, she tried to tell herself, *this is just you imagining things. You'll wake up and things'll be much better then.*

Nodding tiredly to herself, she climbed under the covers and let sleep take her over.

By the time she woke up, the early sun was trickling in through the cracks of the windows. The nauseated feeling had passed, but she was still bloated, with still no blood coming out of her, to her dismay.

Realizing what that could mean, she swallowed and started to worry. If, somehow, her fears were confirmed, Miran wouldn't dare to kill her. Would he? He seemed like too good a man to do that. Then again, he had seemed serious about that condition, and the last man Citrina had been with was—

Maybe, if she could convince him that it happened before their agreement, he could change his mind. But would that work?

Even if those fears came true, she could try to find someone to take it out of her. However, those practices were frowned upon in these areas, despite the many children already dying in the streets, children much like those that the Phoenix took under its wing and helped. Besides, oftentimes the mothers themselves would die of the infections and wounds inflicted by the operation.

Only one option was left—to run away and leave her position. Disappearing would be better than Miran finding out. Sure, there would be speculation, but given her choices, the former seemed like a better, surer alternative. Plus, while it would compromise this specific mission, she had managed to make it this far without anyone, even Jasper, knowing about the Phoenix and her affiliation with it, so she wouldn't be putting her people at risk. Even after a child, she could still try to serve their mission. She could bring up the child to serve with her, if fate were to be kind.

But would it be right to bring up a child in the service? To brand it and mark it, without any regard for whether it wanted to live that way? Citrina was brought up in that life, and as those twenty-eight tallies reminded her, she had been willing to take lives to create a better world and take down the powerful who had turned away aid to people like her when they needed it the most.

Yet, if something, or more accurately, some*one* needed her, it would be hypocritical of her to give the child to someone else, expecting another to take care of what was her responsibility without knowing what would become of it. It'd make her as bad as, if not worse than, the kind of people the Phoenix despised.

She pulled back the covers and looked out the window, seeing a piece of the castle in her view. She could leave within a matter of hours if she needed to, reaching Lumina in a few days' time to ask her what to do, and it was probably better to do so sooner than later.

But was she even sure she was not just having strange bodily changes from an adjustment period? Something in her gut made her want to stay.

She didn't want to admit it to herself, but she did have a fondness for her Lieutenant. She thought it rude to leave without saying anything to him, especially before she was *really* sure what was going on with her. Would she tell him of her suspicions when there might be nothing at all to worry about? Would she act as if nothing happened at all and everything was normal?

Perhaps this was just a side effect of a bleeding that was to come. She shook her head as she re-dressed herself, wondering why she was overthinking what was probably her body's way of acclimating to a new environment, mixed with an improper emotion for the wrong person. Those feelings still nagged her, but she pushed them down. It wasn't appropriate to entertain them and risk whatever she was establishing with her Lieutenant. If everything went well, she could rise through the ranks more quickly and make her choice of this life over court worth it.

In that case, she decided, maybe creating a bit of space between her and Jasper wouldn't be the worst thing. Focusing on improving her skills as a soldier would prove her loyalty to the kingdom in the eyes of her superiors. Besides, the Prince might finally leave her alone about it. She hoped the previous incident proved a point to him, but just in case, she determined she would make sure he had nothing to use against her.

Walking out of her door, she strolled down the hallway and into the big, open courtyard, joining some of the soldiers for a practice and avoiding eye contact with Jasper.

TWENTY-FOUR

LETTA

———

Letta woke up to an empty room and an empty bed. Based on her experiences from the night before, she shouldn't have been surprised, yet she couldn't help but feel disappointed.

Even more so, she missed her family. She rushed to the window to see whether their carriage was still there, but the sun blinded her upon drawing back the curtains. It seemed that she had slept in late and missed her family's departure.

Sighing, she wished she had been able to spend more time with her sister and talk to her. While she had always thought they were complete opposites, Letta still knew her sister loved her deeply, and it was mutual, even if the Princess herself wasn't very good at showing it. The only person here that she felt even slightly close to was her mother-in-law, who had gone out of her way to show a genuine, warm kindness to Letta in her free time, something that she appreciated very much.

Yet the Queen had her secrets as well. The Princess could understand that, but she thought at the very least she could be told *something* rather than being kept in the dark about her new husband's whereabouts and left all on her own, especially on their wedding night.

Turning around, she pulled the covers to make her bed, tidying up the sheets so it would look nice and not tangled up, but the order didn't give her the same satisfaction it usually did. With her hands on her hips, she looked across it, wondering what was wrong. The bed was neat, for sure, but it still felt empty. It was all hers, but it wasn't supposed to be. She was supposed to wake up to her husband, and still, she hadn't seen him since he and the noblemen in the family disappeared from the banquet early.

Shifting her gaze, however, she noticed something on the bedside table—a book with a white rose peeking out from under the leather cover, laid delicately. How long had that been there? She couldn't recall seeing anything of the sort last night.

Pacing over, she lifted the cover to find a handwritten note inside as well.

Letta, my love—please do forgive me for my absence. There was an unexpected emergency to attend to, and we didn't want you to spend such a beautiful night worrying.

I wish I could have danced with you and held you in my arms as your eyes closed for the night. You look so beautiful when you sleep. I imagine your mind is even more so.

My apologies if you have read this already, but it is a favorite of mine. I hope you love it, and I hope to have the chance to talk about it with you.

It was a sweet note, and perhaps he could be forgiven, especially with such a lovely token. She looked at the ornate, gray cover—*The Last Day of the Balaur*—and was surprised that she hadn't at least heard about it. Tucking the delicate white rose behind her ear, she sat on the nearby chaise and gently opened the book.

It was worn from use, signaling that it really must have been one of his favorites. Letta smiled at the thought. Even though she hadn't seen much of her Prince, she felt more connected to him than ever right now while turning the pages to a book that had captured his love.

The book *was* enticing. She found herself flipping through the pages and unable to stop as she read about the adventures chronicling the Marestran Princes and their heroic conquest of a balaur. She admired the pictures of the beautiful yet deadly creature, with its silver batlike wings and seven serpentine heads. Its long, scaly necks and glowing eyes gave her chills even just drawn out in ink. It was hard to imagine the bravery it would take to conquer such a beast in real life.

Even if it was just a legend, it was still riveting to read—a story about how it had escaped from the mountains of the Island of Bones, how it had terrorized fields and villages until the Marestran Princes were the only ones brave and competent enough to defeat it.

The mythology of it was fascinating as well, and she read about its lore, just opening up the final chapter of the book when she was interrupted by a few soft *knocks.*

Startled, her head snapped up to see a darkening room. Had she spent the entire day in here reading? It wasn't out of the ordinary for her, but she couldn't imagine what her new family would think of the fact that she'd been so engrossed in the book that she had forgotten to eat.

With her stomach growling, she rushed to put on clothes other than her nightgown. "Just a moment!" she chirped. Slipping into a simple dark-green dress, she opened the door to see her brother-in-law, Kenric.

"E-everything alright in there?" he asked.

She nodded vigorously, trying to compose herself and running her fingers through her hair. "Sorry, got a little distracted."

Kenric looked over her shoulder, and she followed his gaze to the table with the open book before looking back at him. Catching the wry grin on his face, she blushed.

"I see. W-well, I'm here to f-fetch you for your first r-royal dinner."

She arched an eyebrow. "Haven't we all had dinners together?"

"Y-yeah, I mean… j-just first… s-s-since the wedding…"

Nodding, she smiled. So she would have to see her Prince there too. "Just one minute, and I'll be right there."

Kenric nodded awkwardly, and she went back inside to place the rose from her ear onto the book, coiling her wavy auburn hair into a simple bun and slipping into a nicer dress before returning to the door and following him to the banquet room.

By now, she had expected the silence. The Apasian royalty apparently weren't much for talking outside of formal events, not that she minded. Now that she knew her husband was still thinking about her, she held onto a bit of hope, with a small smile on her face. The dark halls seemed a bit brighter, and the wooden carvings they passed by seemed to have a new bit of warmth in them.

They entered the dining hall, where the table was already decked out with food and perfectly placed utensils, salted venison, and splendid fruits. The other four seats filled up— this time, the seat beside Merek left free, presumably for her to take, so she did.

When her eyes met with that of her Prince, she beamed at him, leaning toward him as she whispered, "Thank you for the note. It was very sweet of you."

Merek gave her an awkward smile back but didn't say anything as he looked over to his mother, waiting for her to give the cue.

Dinner continued in the silence that hung over them. While their dining hall was nice, it did seem modest in comparison to their dinner from the previous night, where their guests had been laughing and drinking and dancing. In a way, Letta almost missed it.

"That was quite a lovely ceremony. Was it not?" Davena broke the silence. The men nodded in silence, and she continued, "I cannot say I have seen a lovelier bride since my own daughters got married."

"That's very kind of you to say, Your Majesty," Letta replied, heat filling her cheeks.

"Very true as well! You left your own groom speechless." She beamed.

The Princess looked over at her husband, whose face turned pink at the comment. He nodded stiffly, mumbling something under his breath that even Letta couldn't hear, still avoiding eye contact with the both of them. What had happened to him? Where was that confident, handsome man she'd met that first day who had won her over? Was that artificial charm something his mother forced him to do as well? Letta sighed, picking at her food.

"Is everything alright, my child?" the Queen asked, her large gray eyes full of concern.

The Princess looked back up at her, unsure of what to say. Glancing around, she saw that the King and both Princes also watched her intently. She swallowed and tried to force a smile. "My apologies, I am just not very hungry at the moment." All eyes were still on her, and she took that as a cue to elaborate. "I have been indoors all day. I probably need a quick walk in the garden—"

"No!" all four exclaimed, and Letta jumped in her seat, her eyes widening. She'd never seen so much emotion from all of them at once, much less fear or worry.

Davena cleared her throat and turned to address her daughter-in-law. "Our apologies for the... strong... reaction," she said with an ingratiating smile. "We tend to avoid night-time strolls—as we live near a forest, we tend to have the occasional... creature come out. For safety's sake, we stay inside until there is light out."

"Oh," Letta replied, a bit disappointed. "Are there no guards?"

"There are," the Queen admitted, "but even they try to be safe and stay inside. Consider it an act of caution."

The Princess wanted to ask more, but the rest had moved on and continued eating. Frustrated, she stayed silent, heading back to her chambers immediately after the plates were collected, not optimistic enough to hope her husband would follow.

TWENTY-FIVE

———

She curled up in the dark alley, sobbing and trying to cover herself up with what was left of her own clothing. A small trail of blood trickled down her upper thigh as she tried to block out the pain throbbing between her legs. Softly touching her neck, she flinched, knowing it would be bruised.

"I'll make you good for something," the Denordan man had said in a kind tone to get her alone with him. She had been so stupid, so naïve, so hopeful that someone wanted to help her out of her nightmare instead of making it worse.

Her shoulders heaved with another wave of sobs as her fingers trailed down to the gold chain that was miraculously still around her neck. After all, the man looked rich enough not to need it. She wished Petyr were here to hold her. He would have protected her, kept her safe from the world that had only hurt her thus far. But it seemed all the good men were killed by the evil ones who outnumbered them. The ones left—

"They really do want only one thing. Don't they?" Looking up, the girl saw that the raspy voice belonged to a woman in a low-cut white dress and ragged cloak standing over her. Her black hair, covered by a white headscarf, framed the chestnut complexion that had darkened in the shadows of the alley.

With one hand on her hip and the other playing with metallic disks woven as a necklace, the woman had a blank, almost disapproving, expression on her face, as if she'd seen this a thousand times over. Perhaps she had.

The girl didn't respond, only sobbed a little bit more quietly. The older woman crouched down to look her in the eyes, lifting the girl's chin so they made direct eye contact.

"Not from here, are you? Running from something?" The girl gave no response. "What if I told you I could give you a place to go? Regular food? Power over and protection from men like that?"

"W-what do you mean?" the girl sniffled.

The woman looked her up and down. "This man used your body because you didn't know how to use it yourself," she whispered. "We'll teach you how to protect yourself, to manipulate men—and get them to pay you for it."

The girl's eyebrows furrowed. "W-why would you do that?"

Breaking into a smile, the woman revealed a chipped tooth. "Because it's fun, more so when you see how weak they are. Weaker, even, than you." Pushing on her knees, she stood up from the crouching position. "You'll be safe with us, should you decide to join." She held out a hand in front of the girl's face.

The girl looked around at the odd stray cat that slinked through the musty darkness, the rags and moldy food strewn about, and the feces that peppered the corner. For once, she was being given a choice. Lie alone with torn clothes in the cold alley and wait for the next man to take advantage of her or follow this stranger promising to feed and clothe and take care of her. This woman seemed to be a saving grace in a place where people just a few paces away were laughing and dancing in the light, ignoring suffering people in the shadows and treating them as if they were nothing.

Her gaze shifted back to the woman whose bagged eyes stared back at her, the cracked skin of her outstretched hand not looking very inviting, but who was she to reject it if she had nothing else?

Wiping her tears, she slipped her hand into the woman's, nodding as she was pulled to her feet.

TWENTY-SIX

OTRA

Even though it was the last night of the festival, one that was supposed to surpass all the others in festivities, the lights shone a little less brightly to Otra. For once, the chatter and singing and music seemed like just noise. All she wanted right now was to be in silence.

But she knew she had to be here. She promised Lumina she'd stay for the entirety of the celebrations and leave right after, yet she couldn't find it in herself to pay much attention to her surroundings. All the voices melted into nonsensical chatter with bodies blurring by, her thoughts too cloudy to pay attention to which official was doing what. In fact, there was only one familiar face she wanted to notice, and he was nowhere to be found. How could she have been so stupid? Getting attached this way was only getting in the way of scouting, something she knew would happen but ignored anyway.

It would all be over soon and she could leave. Perhaps it wouldn't feel as strange for her to wake up alone if it wasn't at the Lebirosi inn. She'd go back to her previous life, focusing on the Phoenix and advancing its mission to gain intelligence and carry out the occasional assassination, if need be. Despite the fact that those previous conversations and moments with him filled up her mind—those dark eyes lit up by sun slipping between the curtains, that smile lighting up every town square that had the fortune of seeing it, the regal grace with which he carried himself—she had no choice but to assume she'd made the right decision. After all, her scars served as a constant reminder to herself that all else came second, and there was no turning back.

Avoiding eye contact with others, she shuffled over to one of the outdoor bar tops for some fresh air.

"Rough night?" asked the burly, bright-eyed barman with a pitying smile.

"Just an ale, please," she said, more softly than she intended. But he either had wonderful hearing or an even better intuition because he wasted no time in pouring her drink before attending to other customers.

"I thought you would have left by now," said a voice from behind her, its familiarity nearly drowned out by the noise of the crowd. Turning her head slightly, her heart hammered in her chest as she saw Vitor standing there.

"Surprise," she replied with a tiny shrug, refusing to meet his eyes.

"What are you doing here?" he asked her in a low voice, pivoting around her to sit by her side. But this time was different from the others, with a distance now between them, and not only in a physical sense.

"Same thing I've been doing this whole time," she responded dryly, still avoiding his eyes by taking a sip of her beverage. She observed the barman as he swiftly poured drinks for the other patrons, having perfected it almost to an art form. The silence between her and her former lover hung heavy and dark, despite the noise surrounding them, as she swirled her drink before swallowing more of it.

He sighed, looking down and scratching the back of his neck. Looking out, he lightly smacked the countertop, as if making a split-second decision. "Would you want to dance, one more time?" Vitor asked, almost impulsively.

Finally, she studied his face. He was trying to compose himself and almost succeeded. His face was suave, but she could still see the vulnerability in his large, dark eyes.

She sighed. It was an awful idea to have involved herself with him in the first place—at least to the extent where he knew who she really was—even if he was a good man. But what was she to do? All the information she came for, and more, was already memorized, and she didn't feel up to any more unnecessary scouting. One more dance couldn't hurt. Nodding reluctantly, she cautiously took the hand he offered her. As she let him lead her one last time to the crowded plaza, the laughing couples swirling around them felt almost foreign to her.

He led her just the same as he had before, as if nothing had changed between them. As he spun her around, she felt that exhilarating rush again, the same she realized she craved every time they were apart. Maybe she could work something out with him. Maybe it wasn't too late to figure out what their feelings meant for one another.

As she looked back up at him, however, she noticed his face was unsmiling and his gaze turned away from her. She tried to follow it, but the way he was leading her was too swift to allow her to get a glimpse of what he was looking at.

"Is everything alright?" she asked, trying to read him to no avail.

He sighed, with a wistful, half-hearted chuckle. "I wish I could say it was."

Otra stopped for a moment, her eyes not leaving him. He finally looked back at her, and for a moment she thought she could see pain in those dark brown eyes as he watched her intently, as if he were taking her in for the last time. She felt like the only person in the world, despite the crowd that surrounded them.

Wrapping an arm around her waist, he pulled her closer, and she felt a sharp, growing pressure in her abdomen. Looking down, she saw a blade in his other hand, lodged deep into the flesh above her navel. Otra let out a sharp gasp and took deeper breaths, but the air felt like it wanted to go anywhere but her lungs.

Her vision blurring, she heard only Vitor's low, taut voice whisper in her ear as he leaned in, the light stubble on his chin scratching the side of her face. "The Allied Cities send their regards."

TWENTY-SEVEN

ANGHEL

The entire day, his brother had ignored him. Even when Anghel had stopped by during training in his free time to join in, Jasper acknowledged him only through scoffs and glares. As the practices ended toward sunset, Anghel approached him as the Lieutenant pulled out arrows from their targets while the soldiers emptied out of the area.

"Where's Onyx?" the Prince asked.

His brother refused to look him in the eye. Usually by now, even when they had conflicts, his brother forgave him. Anghel must have really struck a nerve. "Doing whatever it is she does outside of practice. Probably her own training."

"Like you?"

Jasper nodded, and silence followed. Anghel wasn't sure what to say. Maybe he had been wrong about the two of them after all. Had the Prince's hopes for Jasper finally finding someone on his level, especially as similar to him as Onyx, gotten the better of him?

After standing there awkwardly for a few moments, he decided to continue. "You're still mad about last night?"

His brother looked around as if to make sure no one was around and then glared at him before looking back at his task. "Why would I *not* be?"

"I guess her lack of reaction upset you a lot. Didn't it?"

The Lieutenant pulled out an arrow so aggressively that the target wobbled. "It's a matter of respect for others. That was incredibly indecent and embarrassing for both of us—for me as her superior, for her as a lady…" His gaze dropped, and he muttered, "For us as friends." Shaking his head, he looked back up at the Prince. "That was low."

"But—"

"Even for what I'd expect from you."

Anghel felt a pang in his chest and tried to deflect the insult with a scoff. "I've seen what she can do. I'm not sure that 'lady' is a fitting description for her."

Jasper took a deep breath as if to compose himself. Anghel had never seen him so upset. The closest time he could think of was when they were seven, when his father had taken little Jasper in to make a family of three again, and Anghel had asked where he was from.

"Regardless of what you'd call her, it's inappropriate for her to go to her Lieutenant's private chambers and be invited to see something like that. Situations like that undermine my authority. So perhaps you should stop dragging me along to your little charades with the Sergeants too."

The Prince felt a bit of shame as he looked down at his feet for a moment, racking his brain for a justification, but he couldn't pretend he didn't see the problem now. "Look, I did not mean to cause harm. I just thought something strange was going on. I see the way she looks at you, and my curiosity got the better of me."

His brother looked at him incredulously, those hazel eyes searching his face. "Some curiosity you've got. Even if you hadn't imagined it, she'd be hanged for treason if anything happened. Father's idea, remember? Considering the last woman he knew to get… involved with a soldier, why would you try to make it harder for everyone?"

Anghel clenched his fists, his blood boiling at his brother's audacity. He didn't need to go into detail to bring back that image of the fate that woman had met, bleeding out in the hidden alleys, and the tears his father had tried to hold back in telling his son the truth of what happened, years later. Looking down, he took a few deep breaths. Jasper wasn't the sort to bring these up out of nowhere. He had a reason for it.

"You really care for her, don't you?"

Staring blankly into the target, Jasper stopped for a moment and then nodded slowly. "She's the best we've got."

Oh, thought Anghel. It all seemed so clear to him now, looking back—the way Jasper looked at her as she walked away, the way he was transfixed by any mention of the woman. As the Prince opened his mouth to speak, he was interrupted by one of his father's servicemen gingerly peeking his head from one of the doors to the yard. "Your father requires your presence at the moment, sir."

Anghel looked back at his brother, who was still staring at the targets and refusing to look at him, and then sighed and followed the man.

The servant led him to the throne room to find his father standing and staring at the blackbird banners. Miran nodded at the servant, dismissing him, and approached his son.

"Is everything alright, Father?" Anghel asked, wondering what was so important that the two of them had to be alone.

His father was just a couple of inches shorter, but his stern expression was still enough to scare him straight, just as it did when he was younger. The fact that Miran's face was turning red with fury jolted him as well.

"As you know, you are my heir," the King said in a crisp, strict voice, looking up at his son. "And I cannot have you acting in such a childish manner as you seem to insist on doing."

Anghel opened his mouth to try to protest, but before he could get a word in, his father interrupted.

"Yes, I know what happened. Jasper does not often tell me about your antics. He usually leaves me to guess at them. But it was too far even for you. And even if you thought you were being nice by buying him one of your... trusted *whores*... it was still *unacceptable* for you to have a woman, especially a respectable one who has vowed *in my name* to stay chaste for the sake of the kingdom, watching that obscenity." He kept his voice even, but it steadily grew in intensity, even if he managed to somehow not yell.

"Father—"

"As I mentioned," his father sighed, the disappointment seeping powerfully through in his voice, "you are my heir, and you will be King one day, likely sooner than you think. Padaure needs a King with morality, with decency, one that is not willing to do such... crude... things."

Anghel opened his mouth but wasn't sure what to say. He'd endured talks with his father, but he'd never been berated this extensively.

"So pull yourself together and look nice," his father continued. "You are to be married to Lady Atora, the second daughter of Duke Aurel."

"*What?*" This all seemed like it was coming out of nowhere. Was there not just a wedding in that family? And even if there hadn't been... "Why is this the first I hear about my own wedding?"

Miran ignored his son's reaction. "She is quite pretty and intelligent, from what I hear, and one who is likely too good for you, but perhaps that will be a better incentive for you to at least *try* to be a real man."

Again, Anghel tried to protest, but his father put his hand up to silence him. "This marriage will only serve to strengthen Padaure. As you know, this is a powerful and trusted family in our kingdom. They will be here within the next three days."

"*This soon?* I'd at least expect more of a warning!" Anghel, in disbelief, managed to get out. How could all this have happened so quickly and all behind his back? "Why did you not bother to ask me?"

"You are twenty-two years of age, my son, and you are wasting your strongest years with trashy women and drunken stupors. Had you bothered to mature enough, I would take your opinion seriously and maybe even give you the crown. Most men have multiple children by the time they reach your age. It is time for you to follow suit."

"Maybe I—"

"Bastards do not count."

Anghel sighed, and Miran continued, "Lady Atora will arrive in three days' time, and you are to be married in four. You will dress in your finest attire then, and you will be *nothing* but respectful to our guests and *especially* to your future Queen. No more whores, no more arriving home drunk, no more... scenes... like that of yesterday. You will be my second-in-command until I deem you competent enough to rule on your own.

"Perhaps a wife will teach you to assume responsibility for yourself personally and to stop acting like a child." The King took a deep breath. "One way or another, women have a wonderful way of turning us into the men we're supposed to be."

Both were silent, and Anghel looked over at the banners, staring at the sigil under which he had grown up. As much as he hated to admit it to himself, his father was right. The usual age of coronation was eighteen, and by that definition, he supposed he was behind most men. But his father was doing such a wonderful job on his own. Wasn't he? Besides, the Prince himself wasn't kept up enough to have any real experience, but was that a bad thing? The happy hazes of ale varieties and indistinguishable women were much more fun than shadowing his father and learning about the "subtleties of power."

"Do you understand, my son?"

Anghel looked back at his father, noting the weariness in his eyes and nodding somberly. Perhaps it really was time to let go of his best days.

TWENTY-EIGHT

CARNELO

———

Strolling through the cobblestone streets, past the small clay houses in the town as the sun set, Carnelo draped a stag's pelt over his shoulder as he knocked on the door of one of the neighbors' cottages—his last stop to a customer before he could call it a night.

"Thank ye', sir," the older, shorter man who opened it said, looking up at Carnelo and giving him a smile that revealed a missing tooth. "How goes 't?"

"Cannot complain myself, Aloys, just goin' through the rounds," Carnelo replied, as the man dropped a few coins into his hand.

"Ye' still considerin' tha' move to Monvest?" Aloys asked in a whisper.

The younger man smiled, looking down and pocketing the money. Yes, the man had a knack for learning people's true wishes—and truly, he had gotten Carnelo to reveal his wish, to live as someone else, other than that scarred tall youth who ran errands in the town, to love and provide for a woman, as if any would take him with those ugly scars that ran up his chest and neck.

With a chuckle, Carnelo looked back up at him. "That's for another life."

Aloys grabbed his hand, placing another coin in. "Yer' not very old, Car," he said, looking at the youth intensely and closing the young man's fingers around it. "If you were me, you'd've th' excuse. Go. Soon. Before it's too late to be who ye' want. Y' 'ave the money now, or at least 're close to 't."

"Aloys, I can't—"

"Ye' can, and will—yer' a looker, despite tha' neck. A' least consid'r it."

Carnelo sighed, deciding to pocket that coin as well. "I appreciate it."

Aloys gave a hearty laugh. "Ye' better put 'at t' good use."

"I will." The youth smiled. "Promise."

With a nod, the older man closed the door, and Carnelo looked up to see the sun starting to just barely touch the horizon. His smile grew as he saw the kids who played in the street run inside for dinner, reminding him of a simpler time.

The twelve-year-old boy had just managed to jump up on one of the roofs. After all, his adoptive mother had pleaded him not to, a challenge to any boy that age. "Whoa!" he exclaimed softly, as he climbed over the edge of the house and felt the stiff straw underneath, leaning back so he wouldn't slide down the slant.

He looked over and saw the town from a whole new view. The marketplace was now lit up only by the occasional lantern but emptied out of the merchants by day. Children and adults alike had gone inside, the only sign of life being the light that flooded out of the windows.

"You can fly?" a young girl asked.

His eyes traveled to his left to see the castle, which once had seemed so large to him, but now he felt like he was on top of the world, like he could climb even that. The windows seemed mostly empty, some lit up by small lanterns, some not.

Then he caught her eyes. A young bright-eyed girl leaned out the window not even one story above where he was, staring at him incredulously. After he realized she was the one who had called to him, he laughed. "What if I could?"

Her wondrous eyes widened. "Wau! Can you fly even up to here?"

Shaking his head, Carnelo let out another laugh. "Not sure 'bout that."

"Bet you can," she said. "I'll call you Zbura. Like the one who could fly in the story."

His eyes furrowed. "What? I don't know what story you're talkin' about, but that's not my name."

"It is now. You're the only one I've seen fly!"

He walked over to see her more clearly. Only a few yards away now, he could see her thick, dark hair braided up, and those large eyes so clear they looked as if the moonlight that hit them had given them their color. "If you insist, my lady," he acknowledged, giggling along with her. "And what would your name be?"

He looked forward to this next visit with Atora. She had just returned from her sister's wedding and likely needed comfort. He was more than happy to accommodate and be there for her.

"Didja hear 'bout the young'un?" one of the older ladies gossiped to another on a bench, adjusting her headscarf as he walked by.

"No?" replied her friend, crossing her arms and turning back to the other woman, leaning in. "What 'bout 'er?"

"Duke's marryin' 'er off too."

Carnelo stopped in his tracks. They couldn't be talking about Atora. Could they?

"No! This early?"

"Can hardly b'lieve it me'self," she chuckled. "If he's so good a' marryin' people, maybe he could marry off me useless oaf 'f a boy to a good'un if I ask nice."

He took a deep breath and continued pacing as the women laughed behind him. This must have been just gossip. After all, there had *just* been a royal wedding. The Duke wouldn't be so willing to marry off his last daughter so soon. Would he? Or even if he was, what was the chance he'd be able to work out two arrangements in such a short time? He had a reputation as an efficient man, but even *he* had to have his limits.

When Carnelo stepped through the window and sat on the sill across from Atora, he saw something new—a bag for packing, lying by her bed.

"Is your sister back here on a visit?" he asked, hopeful that she would assuage his fears.

Atora giggled, almost as if she'd forgotten about her sister. "Actually, no," she replied. "I'm leaving tomorrow. I am to marry the Prince of Padaure! My father really does know what's best, doesn't he, Zbura?" She squealed excitedly, twirling around and plopping herself on the bed, her feet taking turns tapping on the floor, as they always did when she was excited.

Does he really? How was this decided so quickly? It'd apparently taken months for the Duke to arrange her older sister's Apasian marriage. How had it happened so quickly for the Prince of their own kingdom?

As she prattled on, running her hands along that thick, dark brown braid that went down to her hips, he tried to brush off his doubts and be happy for her. He really did. She was so sweet, her pure laugh untainted due to the ignorance of the horrors of the real world that lay beyond the view of her window. Atora was still just a girl. She'd never witnessed what humans were truly capable of: death and destruction, malice and malevolence, atrocities and abuse. Her eyes still viewed the world as good and other people as trustworthy, never having to question their intentions because it had never directly affected her beforehand—she always had her castle and guards and father to protect her.

Carnelo would have envied her had he not been entranced by her very being, the sort he'd longed to have remained. He wondered what it would be like to have that childlike innocence again, the memory of which was a tiny shrivel among his childhood of burnt houses and alienating wilderness, stumbling through streets on the hunt for food scraps until a stranger would be kind enough to take him in.

Atora? Life was simple for her—so simple she'd bury herself in romantic stories over and over again to distract herself from the boredom that might otherwise ensue, constantly daydreaming about marrying a Prince who would sweep her off her feet. She never learned to fathom anything else, another life. Why would she? The way she saw it, the things she didn't know were probably more splendid than the life she was used to. Little did she know how wrong she would be, if she were to leave that false paradise.

She walked over to join him at the window, sitting across from him, her mouth moving but none of the words registering in his mind. Instead, he thought of how her life would change the moment she stepped into the Capital. Her lovely eyes would widen upon seeing its sheer size, her jaw would drop and her hands would giddily clap together seeing whatever magnificent castle lay ahead.

The commoners would snicker. Rumors among the kingdom's common folk, especially the ones he'd heard on his rare visits to clients in the Capital, had it that the Prince was a special, and frequent, brothel guest. They even offered him a lower price—maybe due to his royal status, his good looks, or both. The rumor itself varied.

But whether or not it was true didn't matter. The locals would pity this poor, innocent girl for her oblivion to it regardless. By the time she would be self-aware enough to realize that not everyone saw the royals favorably, she would be in for a disturbing turn of conscience.

Commonfolk aside, the royal family would undoubtedly host an extravagant yet traditional maiden's dance for her the night before the wedding, and he imagined how her clear blue eyes would sparkle at how elegantly decorated the hall would probably be. She would at least have a splendid time dancing, and perhaps so would everyone else. Her smile was the sort to light up a room.

Meanwhile, the men in the room would eye her, hoping not to get caught staring while imagining what she looked like under her dress and envying the Prince for being the only prick who would see her like that.

On her wedding day, she would look stunning in her black-and-white gown, surrounded by flowers before her dearest Prince would deflower her and take her first piece of innocence.

No, Carnelo could not envy her or bear to even think about it too much. Her wedding day, at the latest, would likely be her last day of peace before she'd find out about her husband's reputation and realize that perfect Princes didn't exist outside of the pages of a book, before her naïve faith in the purity of others would collapse, before she'd bear children and dread how much like him they would become.

He wanted to warn her, but what would be the point? Carnelo would only come across as pessimistic and maybe even jealous, not as the friend she could always rely on to share pieces of her life with.

Besides, it'd be too late to change anyone's mind. He was nobody, a commoner who had luck only in befriending the Duke's daughter but still invisible to the Duke himself. And this marriage was already arranged. From what he knew of her father, there was no changing his mind once he made a decision. Carnelo was powerless and could only try to hide the pain that struck his heart as he watched her fantasize about what awaited her in the Capital.

He reached over to brush a strand of wavy hair behind her ear, caressing her smooth, porcelain cheek as his fingers traced along her soft jawline. Atora stopped talking and looked at him, puzzled. He leaned in, before fully realizing what he was doing, and found his lips moving onto hers, brushing them just for a quick moment before his conscience pulled him back.

The soon-to-be Princess stared back at him, and to his dismay, he detected no romantic feelings to amplify, only the shock and confusion from what had just taken place.

This time he didn't even bother to try diminishing those emotions for her. He had let his own get the better of him, and he deserved every chance of her potential resentment toward him. Who was he to decide how she felt, especially when it was obvious she didn't consider him in that regard at all, and that as royalty, she never would for a commoner like him?

Jumping down to one of the nearby rooftops, he ignored her calls for him to wait and come back. Carnelo kept running, not bothering to look back.

TWENTY-NINE

———

"Over there," Nerica pointed out, jutting out her chin. *The girls
turned around and saw a plump yet well-dressed older man
sitting on one of the stools at the inn. In the westernmost town
in the Ports of the South, the salty smell of the sea seeped into
the bar.*

"Who is he?" *Amice asked. She was a brunette in the group,
not more than a year older than the others, but with much
more experience, and the sort to take every opportunity to
show that off to the group.* "I can take him."

*Nerica tucked a hair behind her ear and readjusted her
headscarf. She looked past Amice and straight at the blonde
girl, who got an uneasy feeling in her stomach as the woman's eyes bore into her the same way they had in the alley
just a few months prior. She had kept all her promises, and
more—fed her, clothed her, and taught her the tricks of the
trade. But the girl had also learned that nothing came for
free, either.* "He's one of the owners of this Port. I think you
should take him."

*The girl swallowed, looking back at him. The others she'd
had were younger, slightly more attractive, and often leaner,
but she knew that was a kindness for being the newest one. No*

doubt she would be doing most of the work with this client, but hopefully, the money would be enough to satisfy the group, as they pooled the money together for clothes and food.

She knew this was Nerica's test of how worthy she was to remain in the group, and she had to go through with this. Where else did she have to go but their dusty cart? Starving on the streets? Kicked at and raped again? At least here she got something out of it, the chance to have a reliable source of food and clothing while traveling and seeing more of the world as she and Petyr had always dreamt, even if under different circumstances.

The man's sallow cheeks and folding skin didn't make him any more appealing. But he would no doubt pay a higher premium, especially for a young girl like her, and a blonde one at that. It was rare to see a blonde in the Ports of the South, so men might be willing to pay as much as double for one.

Taking a deep breath, she tried to ignore Amice's narrowed eyes as she walked over to the man, plastering a smile on her face. She mustered up all the courage she could, pretending she didn't find him repulsive as she adjusted the cut of her top down to reveal more of the cleavage she'd developed and leaned beside him on the bar, trying to ignore the stench of ale and fish. Batting her eyes, she met his gaze and gave him a smile.

"Good evening, sir," she said in her best mock-coy voice, trailing her hand along his thick arm. She felt the soft silk a girl like her could only dream of affording a sliver of one day. While he was neither attractive nor classy, he had money, no doubt about it.

He smiled, revealing a couple of gold teeth and snaking an arm around her waist. "Well, hello there, young lady."

She tried not to flinch. "Are you busy tonight, m'lord?" she asked politely.

"Not too busy for a beauty like you," he said, his eyes trailing down her body, "and I take it you wouldn't mind doing an... extra... thing or two for a higher coin."

She wanted to ask what, but she didn't want to risk losing her client. Glancing back, her eyes found Nerica's across the bar and were met with a nod and a sly smile, with a hint of pride. Looking back at the man, she nodded, grabbing his hand and leading him around the back of the bar, to the secluded gentleman's room.

THIRTY

LETTA

The books were fascinating, and they kept her mind active, but she could only spend so much time cooped up in that lantern-lit room, and she had more than her share of solitude in the castle. What she once craved back home now evolved into an almost-suffocating loneliness.

She still hadn't seen her husband step into their chambers, and she resolved to cease speaking to him at dinnertime. He didn't bother to start any conversation either, despite the fact that she kept getting notes from him. As beautifully as he had written them, it still didn't replace the neglect she felt from nights of wandering around the castle trying to find him, asking the servants where he was only to get half-hearted shrugs. She'd even tried leaving a note on her bedside table, asking him for a daytime stroll together—only to have it disappear with no answer.

What sort of husband was he—not even fully a husband! They had yet to consummate or spend any time alone together since the wedding. Why couldn't he have gotten his mother's social skills or confidence?

Frustrated, she looked out at the meadow outside her window. The moon looked like just a sliver now, peeking through only the occasional cloud. She could see nothing below besides a peaceful and tranquil garden, and she yearned to get out and soothe herself the way she always did back home.

In a quick moment of rebellion, she decided to go against the family's wishes and head out, grabbing a cloak and shoving the most recent note into one of the folds as she snuck out, looking around to make sure nobody saw her. To her luck, the halls were dark, empty, and absolutely silent.

The lanterns cast a dim yellow light on the light gray path, stone tiles contrasting sharply with the tall, dark hedges that surrounded her as she continued on. Further past the yard in front, the tiles morphed into the soft grass, and the hedges turned to bushes under hanging lights, with the sweet scent of honeysuckle filling her lungs as she admired the various flowers around her—tulips, roses, and many others that she didn't even recognize. Her mother had been right. The garden here was much prettier than the one she was used to at home.

She sniffed the flowers, closing her eyes to hear the clicking of bats and the calls of an owl in the distance. The Princess was glad she'd found a way to get back to a nighttime walk, even if it meant potentially upsetting her new family. The crisp night air soothed her, in combination with the still silence that came with the tranquil atmosphere. This was exactly what she needed.

Would she always feel that sense of empty loneliness, or would he come to her and open up eventually? Looking down to observe a silvery leaf that had fallen in her path, she shook her head. At the very least, she was here alone by choice, and she could breathe out the thoughts that seemed to fill up her room and consume her whenever she was alone inside.

Letta glanced at the beautiful castle behind her, her new home with its tall, dark towers. They looked as if they could just barely reach into the clouds that covered the sky, now concealing the moon so no shimmering beams of silver caressed the balconies.

Turning around, she strolled farther and farther from the castle, wandering through the paths that she couldn't wait to memorize and taking in the whole scene—the multicolored tulips in front of her and the trees of the forest that stood off into the distance as if they replaced the guards that had gone inside, keeping their own secrets of the wild protected from the royals.

Approaching a corner, she heard the faintest rustle and froze in her tracks. The sound ceased, and she stepped forward silently, peeking her head around the hedge to see what could have made it.

About twenty feet away stood a horrid creature hunched over, the likes of which she'd never seen before. Its skin was thin and gray, appearing as if it had been stretched out over its eight-foot frame, with tattered pants covering its lower half. The creature's feet were pointed as if they were made of pegs, and the fingers consisted of long, black, needle-like talons that could easily pierce through flesh.

The monster turned its bald head, hissing but falling silent when it saw her. Letta's breath caught in her throat as its pupil-less dark-red eyes met hers, glowing faintly in the lantern light. The mouth, which had momentarily exposed sharp, skinny teeth with gaps in-between them, closed, and the creature seemed to freeze as well, but that didn't stop her stomach from flipping over. Her conscience screamed at her to run or hide, but her feet felt rooted in place, too petrified to move.

Strangely, the monster started to shrink away, covering its head with its large hands as if trying not to be seen.

Out of a sort of morbid curiosity, Letta found herself taking a step toward it, overcome with an odd sense of compassion for the creature that hunched over more as if to hide. The creature flinched as she took another step, glancing at her and taking a tiny step away. Her fear began to slowly melt away with every new step, and she began to feel more sorry for it as it watched her from between its talons, now not moving at all. If anything, its very form seemed to be shrinking as she stepped closer, and... What was that? Even beginning to sprout hair?

One step slowly followed another, and its talons shrank. When she was just about ten feet away, something shot into its back, jolting it as it let out a screech that sounded almost half-human. Another two bolts flew into it, and the creature collapsed.

Letta rushed over to it, and as she approached it, she found the courage to touch it, watching the creature become more and more humanoid to evolve into a shockingly familiar face. Merek's bare chest had rivers of blood trickling down it from the wounds on his side, and his eyes looked up at Letta with the sort of vulnerability one might see in a scared child.

"I'm—I'm sorry," he choked out.

Letta shook her head, her heart pounding and her breath catching as tears welled up in her eyes, and she froze. This must have been what they were hiding. She could see why. Any person in their right mind would have tried to leave. But yet here she was, holding him in her arms and trying to ignore the blood that seeped onto her nightgown.

Looking up, she followed the trajectory of where the bolts must have come from and could have sworn she saw a familiar figure with a crossbow in hand—a tall, spindly one, the same as that of... Could it be? Yet she only caught him for a moment before he vanished from the window. Had he realized this was his brother and shot him anyway? Had he planned it? Or had he noticed a stalking creature in the garden and tried to protect her?

She felt a shaky hand tap her arm and looked back over at her husband. "Run," his weak voice gasped.

"Away? I can't leave you here."

"H-he'll come—for you," the Prince insisted, sweat droplets running down his temple.

"I won't leave you like this," she argued, her hands traveling his chest and trying to figure out what she could do, but it only resulted in more blood smearing onto her hands.

A tear rolled down her cheek. Slowly, she leaned over and kissed him on the forehead.

He managed a faint smile. "At-at least, your eyes are the last th-thing I'll see," he managed, letting out a last sigh before the life left his eyes. She could only stare at him lying there motionlessly. Of course. He didn't want her to have to see him like this. Who would? Was it now her fault that she had? Was that why everyone in the castle acted so strangely with her? Was that why his brother had killed him?

Glancing back up, she still saw the open balcony windows from where the shot had been taken. There was no doubt that Kenric was either hiding or on his way over. If Merek himself, his own brother, had said he'd come for her next... She couldn't rely on the safety of the castle now, and it seemed too risky to hope to find the Queen first.

It could have been the delirium of a dying man, but she didn't want to take that chance. She took one last look at her husband and caressed his face, leaning over to kiss his forehead again before heeding his final command, lifting her skirt, and running toward the forest.

THIRTY-ONE

ATORA

———

Atora couldn't help but stick her face through the blinds in the carriage to gawk at the Padaurean Capital as she was taken through its winding cobblestone streets. The inns she passed by, with the locals chatting in the street markets down the alleys, reminded her of home, but she didn't feel as homesick as she imagined she would.

Maybe she wouldn't miss her old town. She wondered if Letta felt the same when she had moved to her new home, although Atora was gladder to be here. The castle was closer to the city, and a larger one at that, with more to explore—if her husband would allow her to.

The girl wondered what her future husband was like. She'd heard he was handsome, and the fact that he was a Prince too! Her mind raced with the prospect of that. She would be Queen one day, giving birth to beautiful little Princes and Princesses, serving at court by his side to get lavish gifts from visitors who came from every corner of the Continent. Smiling at the thought, she felt even more elated as they took her through a small arched gate.

The castle loomed over the city with scarlet, cone-shaped towers topping a large stone structure that stood elevated on the hill. It was surrounded by a small valley, the only visible entrance being a long bridge suspended by stone pillars.

While she was taken up the hill, however, she saw that the castle itself was smaller than the one Letta had moved into. From the outside, it looked only about twice as large as the one she grew up in back home, but it was probably because her father was the most prestigious Duke in the kingdom—a longtime, loyal friend of the King's and treated as such. She also noticed a building outside of the castle and asked the servant in the car with her about it.

"That's the soldiers' quarters, m'lady," he responded with a nod.

"The soldiers' quarters?"

The man nodded again. "Yes'm, home to the Capital Royal Guard—too large to fit all in one castle."

She raised her eyebrows for a second, impressed. Admittedly, she'd never thought about that. Sure, her father had guards, but there was enough room in her castle back home for them to sleep as well. It seemed that she wouldn't have to worry about safety, in that case.

The carriage came to a halt, and another servant opened the door, holding out his arm for her to take. Graciously, she stepped out to see a long, tawny bridge stretching over one hundred feet ahead of her and leading to that marvelous stone castle.

As she was escorted in through the arched entrance and large, wooden gate, she was met by a large, grassy courtyard surrounded by two stories of stone arches and walls and decorated by the blue blackbird banners of the kingdom. A stern older man in blue dress intricately embroidered with gold threads walked to her, his curly salt-and-pepper hair furling underneath a thin yet intricate gold crown.

"Your beauty far exceeds what words can give justice, Lady Atora," he said with a kiss on her hand, his kind lavender eyes lighting up. "Your father and I have been very excited to arrange this."

She smiled, her heart filling up. Her King calling her beautiful *and* already approving of her? This had to be a good sign. But she had to heed her mother's advice and be modest. "You truly do honor me, Your Majesty."

The King nodded and turned to his servant, a scrawny, mousy-haired man beside him who had been helping other servants fetch Atora's belongings from the wagon. "Do you know where Anghel might be?"

"I'll fetch him, Your Majesty," the man replied, and the two exchanged nods.

"No need for that," a slightly deeper voice said, and the three of them turned to see a tall frame walking their way. His lightly tanned skin shone in the sunlight that flooded in, as did his wavy hair, which resembled spun gold. She noticed the definition of his toned arms through the airy white blouse he wore.

As he walked over, he stood a full head over Atora's petite frame, nodding politely. "I take it you must be Lady Atora." He smiled, taking her hand and brushing his soft lips on her knuckle. "You are even lovelier than the rumors describe."

She couldn't stop the heat from rising to her cheeks at the compliment, nor could she take her eyes off his chiseled jawline or the long, elegant fingers that had shot chills up her spine when he touched her. *This* was her Prince? He was far more handsome than she could have imagined.

Opening her mouth slightly, she just barely managed to croak out, "Pleasure to meet you, my Prince."

Pleasure to meet you? she thought, mentally kicking herself. *You've read far too many romance stories to let that be your first sentence to your future husband.* Yet, her stupid self had let that out. Why couldn't she have been more poetic? He probably thought she was incredibly awkward. She wished she could tell him this wasn't her usual self, that she was normally bubbly and talkative and easygoing, but then again, she didn't normally meet Princes, especially not this handsome.

A short silence ensued, and another servant walked in, carrying the last of her bags. Looking back at the men, she blurted, "I should go unpack my things and get cleaned up."

The corners of the Prince's mouth turned up slightly, and the King nodded. "Be sure to be in the main hallway by sundown for the maiden's dance."

She nodded nervously before slipping away and following the servant to her chambers for the night. The maiden's dance? Atora had completely forgotten about the old Padaurean tradition of celebrating one last dance as an unmarried woman. Her sister hadn't had one, but then again, she was sure the Apasians had their own quirks.

She prayed that she could look good for her betrothed at the dance, as well as her future father-in-law. She *had* to make a better impression on them, and she hoped to do so then. The girl always felt right at home at dances and court events, after trying to make a habit of everything her parents had taught her.

Flipping through the dresses she had packed, a female servant who came to bathe her also helped get her dressed. "It'll be nice to finally have a royal woman in the castle 'gain," the woman gushed as she helped Atora out of the bath. "Gets a bit much with only men 'round here."

"What about the Queen?" the girl asked as the woman patted her down with a cloth.

"What 'bout 'er?"

"Why isn't she around?"

The woman fell quiet, turning around and laying out a few of Atora's dresses on the bed. So it was taboo. While it hadn't done much to quell the future Princess's curiosity, she knew how to take a hint, hoping to find out later on.

Standing in front of the bed, she settled on an azure dress, one that hugged her waist and torso but flowed out a bit more from the hips. It had beautiful black-and-white embroidery with the occasional blue threads stitched into the hem, and she hoped it would be fitting.

Looking into the mirror, she almost didn't recognize herself. Her face hadn't changed at all physically, but with her thick brown hair so intricately braided out of her face and her dress so well-fitted, she felt and looked much older than sixteen—more like a truly mature woman, or at least someone on the way to becoming one. Only a few weeks had passed since her sister had left, but it almost felt as if years had gone by, with everything that had changed. She had no doubt that she was ready for marriage—she'd waited her whole life for this—but still wished her sister was here to see her, even as she understood that there was no way Letta would be able to make it all the way from Apasia in time for the wedding.

"Ready, miss?" the woman asked.

Atora took a deep breath and nodded, whether to herself for reassurance or to the servant, she wasn't sure.

The hall was immaculate with lanterns filling it to create a somewhat rustic, moonlit atmosphere. Elegant dressings in blue lined the walls, and the room was filled with lovely people and energetic music from the band in front. However, as her eyes scanned the room during her royal introduction, she recognized no one. After all, her family would likely not be here until tomorrow.

Taking another deep breath, she put on a smile. She loved this—the idea of dancing with strangers, meeting new people. Something was simply *invigorating* about it.

She felt a light tap on her shoulder and turned to see a lanky, red-haired man, who looked to have a small cut on his jawline, the sort that might happen from shaving. Holding out a hand for her, he began, "Name's Sergeant Osbert, m'lady. Would ye' do me th' honor 'f a dance?"

Softly slipping her hand into his, she nodded. "It is lovely to meet you, Sergeant. My name is Atora."

"So I've heard." He grinned, beginning to lead her. "Yer 'usband-t'-be's one of me best friends."

"Oh," she said. "Are you—?"

"Not a Prince, if ye' couldn' tell." He chuckled. "Jus' a Sergeant."

"I did not realize nobility and guards were so close."

"Usually i'nt, but his brother's my Lieuten't, an' we're a good lil' family 'f our own." He nodded.

"A Prince can be a Lieutenant too?" She was confused. While her father had held command of the forces in the area, he would still designate someone else to watch over the training in such a role.

He shook his head again. "More 'f an… adopted… son of the King's. Some orphan th' men found while huntin' years ago an' took pity on." The Sergeant nodded to himself. "Good man, though, an' damned best 'f all 'f us."

"Remarkable." Atora had never heard of a nobleman *adopting* a child. They usually were too preoccupied with trying to make and raise their own to pass on the royal bloodline. The more she learned about this place, the more she realized she didn't know as much about the royalty as she had previously thought. But the Capital seemed to be full of only good surprises. If the King himself was so kind, she could only imagine how sweet her Prince was.

The song ended, and Osbert bowed. "Thank ye' for th' dance, m'lady. Anghel's a lucky man." He winked.

"You are very kind to say, sir," she replied sweetly. Although his speech gave him away as a lower-class man, she was impressed that he had risen up the ranks to be a Sergeant. He reminded her of her dear friend that she'd left behind at home. She pushed the thought out of her mind. This was a happy occasion, even if it did come at the cost of leaving on strange terms with him. That's what a real lady would do—carry on and be happy wherever she found herself.

"Ye' must be thirsty. 'ad any of the wine yet?" Osbert offered. "They save this stuff fer th' best 'ccasions."

She hesitated before admitting, "I cannot say I would know good wine from bad."

He looked at her incredulously. "Ye've never 'ad a drink?"

Atora shook her head. "Father was always strict—said a lady should know how to hold herself well."

The Sergeant chuckled. "A sip won't do ya' in." He handed her a glass.

Swirling it around like she'd always seen royal women do, she took a whiff of the fermented grapes, letting the sweet scent fill her senses. Taking a sip, she found it was slightly more sour than she had expected, but she didn't mind. She liked the taste and the warm feeling in her chest from it.

She wasn't sure what gave her the courage, but she found herself asking about the Queen.

Osbert looked around. "Good thing ya' asked me an' not one o' th' others." He chuckled nervously.

She raised an eyebrow, prompting him further.

His eyes darted around, as if trying to make sure no one was listening. The band was playing, and people still had cheerful smiles on their faces, dancing gleefully around them and not paying as much attention to them as she would have expected. He leaned over, speaking to her in a hushed tone. "She died sixteen years 'go, when Anghel was jus' a tot."

"That is awful," she replied, keeping her voice low as well. "What happened to her?"

He took a deep breath, looking around again before turning back to her. "Rumors 'ave it she got pregnant from a soldier. Tried to get rid 'f it, but it went sideways. By th' time they found 'er in the alley, she'd lost too much blood."

Atora stared blankly at the dancers in the middle of the room, not quite sure what to say. Did everyone else know as well? If they did, she couldn't say she wondered why they had been so hush-hush about the Queen.

"Didn't hear 'bout it from me," he continued, taking a sip of his drink and also looking around the room.

"Of course not," she responded, as the song ended and he walked off. She couldn't imagine what this family must have gone through, the horror of the broken vows, the pain of a woman—especially a wife and mother—who had gotten herself killed rather than facing the consequences. She wanted to comfort the King and her Prince, to hug them and be there for them, but what would she say now? It was too long ago, maybe even around the time she was born, and it'd probably only open old wounds.

"May I have this dance?"

Atora turned toward the familiar voice to see her old friend Zbura standing there, hand outstretched in a simple white blouse and dark trousers. He looked cleaner than she was used to seeing him, his curly dark locks parted out of his olive-toned face.

"Zbura! What are you doing here? How did you—?"

"I flew," he joked, winking at her. Gingerly, she took his hand, surprised to see him here, now, at her maiden's dance over a hundred leagues away from home. After all, the last time she'd seen him was three days ago, the night before she left, when he kissed her and ran away. She hadn't figured out how to comprehend the situation but was able to push it out of her mind with everything else happening. But seeing him here now, she wondered... Had he, her lifelong friend at the window, traveled all this way just for her?

He pulled her close, as he led her with swift, graceful maneuvers, their faces inches away from each other. Where had he learned to dance?

Standing here now, in an unfamiliar place with unfamiliar people, she thought about the one familiar face in front of her. Then she realized she still hadn't much of an idea what he did outside of the time they spent together, despite knowing him for so long. How well did she *really* know him? How rude had it been to not take the time to even ask, despite his claims that his life was boring?

Her heart felt like it was on fire, and the taste of his breath mixing with hers seemed to fill her tired lungs with life. Yet his face betrayed no vulnerability. If anything, he acted as if it were natural for him to be there, with her in his arms, and she did her best to go along with it, looking down at her feet to try to make sure she could keep up.

As the song began to slow down, she looked up from her feet into his emerald eyes, which looked as if they were glowing among the lights that surrounded them. He leaned in closer, his lips almost touching her ear. "You look beautiful. I hope the Prince knows how lucky he is," he whispered.

Her cheeks flushed, and she opened her mouth to speak, but no words came out, whether out of shock or lack of breath from his quickened pace, she couldn't figure out.

In the blink of an eye, right as the last note of the song played, he seemed to have disappeared. Another man asked her to dance, this time the King, and she tried to keep her attention on whatever he was saying. However, she found that her gaze kept scanning the room, searching in vain for those familiar dark locks and wondering whether the wine had made her imagine the whole thing.

Later that night, Atora sat by the window, staring at the rain that had started to fall. By this time tomorrow, she would no longer be in the chambers of a maiden but in the arms of her Prince—a man more beautiful than she could have dreamed—tall with vivid lavender eyes, flowing blond hair, and skin appearing smoother than silk. So why did something feel… off?

Cracks of white pulsed through the sky, lighting up the whole city below her, and she was taken back to another, simpler time.

A flash of light filled up the room and then disappeared just as quickly as it had come. A loud rumble seemed to shake the room. The little seven-year-old Atora whimpered, shaking under the blanket.

"Why do they scare you so much?" asked the older boy sitting on the windowsill. "You don't find them... how'd you put it... fascinating?"

Peering over the covers, she shook her head violently.

"Why not?"

"They're bad luck, and bad things always happen with them."

He chuckled and made his way over. "In the books?"

She nodded.

The boy sat down by her side, smelling of the rain that had started just moments before he'd leapt in. "Maybe in those stories but not in yours."

"How do you know?" she challenged, starting to move out over the covers to sit by his side.

He put a damp arm around her, and she began to calm down. "I'm here. As long as I'm here, I won't let anything bad happen to you. I promise."

THIRTY-TWO

The tavern was smaller than the sort she was used to, but then again, her party usually stuck to large cities, only passing through villages on the way to others. They were only here for the night before passing on to Padaure.

However, she saw a handsome, dark-blond man at the bar, one she hadn't expected to see in a secluded mountain village like this. He looked relatively young, not much older than her own age of twenty, with dark stubble covering his face like a shadow and a certain light in his dark eyes.

Ignoring the chatter among her party, she decided that even though it was their night off, she could still try to enjoy herself and perhaps even make a quick coin.

Slinking along, she swung her hips slowly and seductively. After three years of experience, she had it down to a science, the technique coming along naturally.

She gently moved beside him and decided to play coy, pretending not to notice him at first. He paid her no attention, but she could be patient. As she sat down, he turned and had just opened his mouth to say something when she felt a tap on her shoulder. Turning around, she found a young, doe-eyed woman with curly caramel hair, holding a few drinks.

"Hello, miss," she said sweetly, "pardon me, but you seem to be sitting in my spot."

Looking around, the girl saw both her and the man's eyes on her, and she shifted one seat away from the man, flustered. "My apologies," she said flatly, offering an insincere smile.

"No need to apologize!" the woman said, chipper as she set down the drinks on the countertop. "You must be new in town. I haven't seen your face around here."

The man joined in, his eyes full of affection as he looked at the curly-haired woman before speaking back to the girl. "She really is good with faces," he added, placing an arm around the caramel-haired woman. "This is my wife Jade, and I'm Chryso." He extended a hand out to her. "And you are?"

The girl looked back at her party of half-dressed girls. The only one who seemed to notice her was Amice, who gave her a sarcastic smirk as if to say, "Trying to catch a married man. Nice one." The blonde girl turned back to the couple. Should she tell them her name?

Chryso seemed to note her apprehension and retracted his hand as Jade followed where the girl's gaze had been.

"Those your friends?" she asked.

The girl remained silent, unsure of what to say. They were just other girls who were looking to make a quick coin and had nowhere else to go. She couldn't say she necessarily considered them friends, only cheap company. She elected for a hesitant shrug.

Jade laid a soft hand on her shoulder, looking her up and down before looking into her eyes, and the girl felt entranced by their color. She could see why Chryso looked at her the way he did. It was almost as if her eyes were themselves made of granite, gray with flecks of hazel and white in them.

"You can tell me the truth," she whispered. "Do you want to go back to them?"

Looking back at the group one more time, and then quickly back at Jade, she gave her a vigorous shake of the head, not sure why she could feel tears filling up her eyes. Twisting the chain on Petyr's necklace, she tried to remember the last time she was as bubbly and happy as this woman seemed to be. Why had she admitted to this stranger something she hadn't even had the courage to admit to herself?

Jade and Chryso shot each other a look and he nodded. The wife gave the girl a gentle side-embrace, filling her with a strange yet genuine warmth—the kind she couldn't remember feeling, at least not for years, and whispered, "I can make you an offer, one that is completely fine for you to turn down."

The girl glanced at her curiously, cueing her to continue.

"If you would like, you can let your... 'friends'... go ahead without you, and you can stay here with me and Chryso. We'll take care of you until you find your own place to stay. You'll be safe here." Jade took both her hands. "We'd love to help you."

Helping. The girl couldn't remember the last time someone had offered to help her, but this woman seemed too pure, too welcoming for any bad intentions, and was even offering her an escape!

She looked again at the group, and it seemed only Amice had noticed her absence, still glaring back at her. Did she really want to go back and face her? Or Nerica? Or whatever disgusting fellow she'd have to sell her body to again?

Her gaze went back to Jade, whose eyes were filled with... compassion? When was the last time someone had looked at her with such kindness? What was the catch? What would she have to go through?

Sighing, she figured that at least she'd already seen enough darkness and had enough of it done to her that this new risk might be worth it. What did she have to lose?

As she gave Jade a nod, the woman met her with a full embrace and ordered another drink from the innkeeper, placing the warm brandy in front of her and accompanying it with an even warmer tone in saying, "Welcome to Auremont."

THIRTY-THREE

JASPER

———

The Lieutenant found Citrina at the tiny hideout in the mountain where they had snuck out before. That scene his brother had arranged had played over and over in his head ever since it had taken place. In every incessant reiteration, he tried to recall whether she'd expressed any sort of emotion but failed. They had managed to convince Anghel that nothing was going on—or rather, she had, while Jasper had stupidly let his feelings for her slip afterward.

He understood what was at stake and why she did it. But was she *that* good at hiding her emotions—and if so, just how good was she? Had he just made up the idea that she felt the same about him? Watching her legs dangling off the ledge, he wasn't sure what would be worse.

She seemed to notice him, and she froze before her eyes stared back out over the horizon. As he climbed up, Jasper worried about what they'd hold when he got the courage to look in them up close.

Pulling himself up, he sat beside her, but her gaze hadn't moved and her expression remained blank. She wasn't herself. This Citrina was stiff, frozen, almost empty. Something had gone from her, and he couldn't quite figure out what.

Was that one shameful moment enough to erase every-thing—the hushed conversations and the tender embraces in the shadows?

He reached for her hand, softly brushing his fingers over it. Unexpectedly, she flinched as if he'd never done that before, but finally, she looked him in the eyes. She looked lost, as if she were a little girl stuck on a foreign road—a strange look for the normally self-assured, graceful woman he thought he knew.

"Citrina," he whispered. A little bit of tension seemed to escape from her shoulders, warming up ever so slightly to the sound of her name from his lips, although she remained stiff as she eyed him. "I am so sorry for Anghel's disgusting... indecency. I hope you know that I hated every bit of it. I had no part in planning it, nor would I ever—"

"Jasper," she interrupted, his name sounding like home from her lips, as if they'd never been separated. The feeling that came up in his chest every time she said it was perhaps what cemented their friendship to the depth it had reached— the feeling of an old home that was lost and rediscovered.

Apparently taking the silence from his undivided atten-tion as a cue, she continued. "I understand, and I had to act as if it didn't affect me so as to not draw suspicion, but, well..." She trailed off, breaking eye contact and staring off into the distance as if possessed by the same thought that had consumed her when he found her.

"What is it?" he asked, his chest tingling with dread-ful anticipation.

She took a deep breath and looked him in the eyes. Was that fear in her own? Her gaze dropped, and she softly con-fessed, "I have feelings for you, and... very strong ones at that."

Jasper couldn't help but let out a small chuckle of relief as he scooted closer to her, placing his arm around her. His hand softly held on to her shoulder. "I can only assume you know that is reciprocated."

In the moonlight that shone on the edges of her cheekbones, the corners of Citrina's mouth quirked up, but that expression disappeared as soon as it had appeared. Slipping out of his grasp, she made her way away from the ledge and moved under the mouth of the cave. The shadows shielded her from the moonlight as the rain began to fall.

"And what?" she continued, speaking more slowly than usual, which didn't do much to stop the trembles in her voice that betrayed her anguish. "We can't be together. The King would hang me for treason, and you're like a son to him. Tonight's the maiden dance for the wife he found to suit Anghel, isn't it? I wouldn't be surprised if he might try and find one for you as well."

Jasper followed her and wrapped his arms around her, resting his chin on her head. This time, she slowly melted into his embrace, and he moved his chin just slightly to kiss her softly on the forehead. Despite the rumble of thunder that had started off into the distance, a delicate peace ensued with them standing there, her arms around his waist and his grasp firm, afraid to let her go. He breathed in that linden scent and let it intoxicate him as it filled his lungs, unable to imagine wanting anyone else here with him, the way she was.

He decided to be the one to break the silence with just a whisper. "What if he doesn't have to try?"

Citrina pulled back slightly, and in the shadows, he could barely see her brows furrow. "What do you mean?"

"What if I already found one? A wife, I mean."

"Then why are you here with me and not with her?" She tried to pull away more, but his grip didn't let her. After a few seconds of struggle and his silence as he smiled at her, the idea seemed to finally catch up to her. "W-we couldn't," she stammered. "Didn't I just remind you—?"

His heart raced as the idea grew in his mind, and Jasper let go to take her hands in his excitedly. "I could talk to him, change his mind, Citrina. I mean it. I wouldn't want anyone else. I could even try to convince him to have us married in secret—"

"No," she said firmly, her eyes growing watery, and looked away. She dropped her hands out of his with a sigh. "He was very clear with me. Hell, knowing that this whole thing would be with the *Lieutenant* of his Royal Guard, of all people, he might even put me on the wheel."

"Don't say that, he wouldn't—"

She looked back up at him sternly, a mix of emotions in her eyes that he couldn't quite read. "It's far too risky. I can't say yes to you." She touched his face lightly before dropping her hand, a tear escaping and trailing slowly down her cheek. "No matter how much I want to. I'm sorry."

He stared at her in disbelief. Was she doubting his loyalty? How willing he was to convince the King? She shouldn't be. After all, he wasn't Anghel. Jasper knew the King trusted him. "Citrina," he whispered pleadingly, cupping her face in his hand and wiping away the tear with his thumb, "Trust me. I don't want anyone else."

She smiled halfheartedly, her face briefly lit up by a flash of lightning as she the hand that was on her cheek. Elevating herself slightly on her toes, she brought her lips to his, kissing him with the same passion they had shared on their first night together a few months ago. She held him as if she too were afraid to let go.

When she pulled away, he saw a couple more glistening tears had streamed down her cheeks. She wiped them off herself, lifting on the balls of her feet to give him one last kiss on his cheek before turning around and walking out of the cave, climbing back down and leaving him dumbfounded in the pouring rain.

THIRTY-FOUR

LUMINA

Lumina paced the length of the tent in their current mountain encampment as the lanterns flickered. Her gaze wandered as she observed the light. "Do we have any updates on our sites?" she asked Borin, her second-in-command at the campsite who was just a few years her junior. "Marestra?"

"The youngest of the royal sons is coming up on eighteen, which means that the Festival of the Fights is happening soon," he replied dutifully, his posture straight and his hands clasped behind his back.

"I've heard those are the spectacle of a lifetime," she replied, looking back up at him. "Find out exactly when that's happening. I would love to see that."

"Of course, ma'am."

"What about Apasia?"

"Royal wedding recently, with one of the daughters of Duke Aurel of Padaure, from the northernmost state, according to Herry."

"Interesting. I assume his younger one is to be married soon as well."

"To Prince Anghel of Padaure—the wedding is tomorrow evening."

Lumina smiled, drumming her fingers on the table and taking an interest in the pockmarks on it. "Lovely. We should send a scout to see that and to check on Citrina in the meantime." She hadn't heard from the girl in a couple of weeks, although that was more characteristic of her. The girl's style was to act and live in the moment, but she always worked to improve the standings of the Phoenix.

Borin nodded again. "Noted, ma'am."

After she continued pacing the room in silence for a moment, the leader's eyes widened as she came to a realization. "Hasn't the Festival of the Free finished by now?"

"It has, ma'am," the man replied, "just a couple of days ago, if I'm not mistaken."

"And I have yet to hear from Otra. She should be back by now."

"We haven't heard anything from her in the past week or so," Borin told her.

"*Anything?*" she replied, looking at him incredulously.

He walked up to her and placed a hand on her shoulder, probably to try to comfort her. "I'm sure she must've found something big, something of interest to the Phoenix."

Lumina shook her head. She knew the scout better than that. It wasn't like her to be late without saying anything. "She's never been late," she said coldly, "especially not without sending a bird to let us know."

Borin sighed. "I suppose. Perhaps we can send someone else to check up on her?"

She nodded, pulling a strand of sand-colored hair behind her ear. The sooner they could find out what was going on with Otra, the better. They couldn't afford to lose one of their best to capture, death, or worse... treason. "She wouldn't just vanish unless something happened to her or gave her a reason to go into hiding."

He nodded, his thick brown eyebrows furrowing as he scratched his close-cropped, curly beard.

Tybalt, a fellow soldier who had just been promoted to be the General overlooking Marestran operations, peeked his bald head into the tent. "Pardon me, ma'am. Am I interrupting anything?"

Lumina gave a false smile as she looked at Borin and patted him on the shoulder. "Not at all. Borin here was just giving me a status update. Is everything alright?"

Tybalt had a puzzled look on his face, his broad nose crinkling as if he were unsure what to say, or at least how to say it. "I'm not sure how... but... someone may have stumbled upon the premises..."

Her smile disappeared, and she could feel the blood drain out of her face. "What? How?"

Throwing up his hands in the air cluelessly, Tybalt exclaimed, "I haven't the slightest. The people on watch didn't recognize her."

"Is it a spy? A mole?"

He shook his head. "She seems a bit too... clueless... at least based on the interactions thus far. We've seized her, and she's currently under watch. I thought you might want to know."

Lumina nodded, running her fingers through her hair nervously. What did this mean? She had thought they were difficult to find, a rumor that wasn't more than a whisper in the wind, as she had trained them to be. Did someone let something slip? Who would she have to kill for such treason?

"Bring me to her," she finally said. "I'd like a word."

The General nodded.

"Lumina," Borin called as she walked out. She turned around, watching him shuffle over to her side with worry in his large brown eyes. "Would you like me to accompany you?"

She smiled at him. "I appreciate the offer, but you have more pressing things to do. Go carry them out."

Borin nodded, exiting the tent with the other two and turning out of their sight. Lumina followed Tybalt through the encampment of brown canvas tents, concealed in the heart of the mountains that separated Apasia and Padaure from Denorda and Eputer. The forest was so thick it'd be hard for anyone outside of the Phoenix to find even if they tried—or so they had thought. Perhaps this was a sign they would have to pack up and reestablish their base at another spot again. She sighed. That would be a pain, especially with the stormy weather that had started to roll in, and all of the communication it would take to update their scouts and spies throughout the Continent of the location change.

Peering into a tent, Tybalt motioned with his hand that she was safe to enter. The inside was dark with only one lantern in it and nothing else. An occasional stray leaf floated over the dirt floor, and an implanted pole in the middle held up the tent. A few ropes restrained the girl to the pole, her ankles bound and her hands tied behind her back. It seemed to be a good setup especially for something so last-minute. They didn't often take prisoners.

The girl looked up, her auburn hair glowing red in the faint lantern light, and her eyes, such a light blue that they seemed almost clear, were filled with apprehension. Smears of dirt and blood patterned her pale face, and her simple gray-green dress, which might once have been lovely, was tattered and covered in mud. She was thin and looked tired. Lumina had been right; no way could she be a threat.

"Not very often do we have people stumbling upon us," Lumina mused.

"P-please don't hurt me... I-I told the others, I don't know where I am... or who you are... who anyone here is..." the girl stammered in a thick High Continental accent.

"How did you get here?" the woman asked, tilting her head to the side curiously. How did someone so weak, so clueless, get this far into the forest and make it all the way to the encampment?

The girl looked down at the worn slippers on her crossed feet. "I'm afraid you wouldn't believe me. The others didn't."

Lumina crouched down in front of her, tilting the girl's chin up so their eyes met. "I've seen a lot of things others wouldn't believe. Try me."

Her prisoner hesitated.

"Perhaps start with who you are." The woman looked at her patiently.

The girl stayed quiet, and just as Lumina was about to speak up, she replied, "My name is Letta. Daughter of Duke Aurel of Padaure... and—"

"Princess of Apasia," Lumina finished for her incredulously. Not just any girl stumbling upon their premises but a *Princess*? This had to be a joke.

Letta's brows furrowed. "How did you know?"

"Royal weddings are not exactly secret, even here," Lumina scoffed, rising to her feet and pacing the tent. "So why would a Princess leave her beloved new kingdom... and find herself in these mountains? I take it that you didn't just get lost on a walk."

"I think I was in danger," she confessed.

"More danger than you would be in the wild? Or in a place like this?"

Letta's shoulders dropped along with her gaze, and she looked at her feet sheepishly. "I didn't think it through. I admit it."

"Obviously."

The Princess's gaze fixated on a random spot of dirt, the fear evident in her eyes as her voice dropped to a soft almost-whisper. "But I saw something terrible—so awful that if I weren't here, I'd think I was having a nightmare."

"Do tell," Lumina prompted curiously. "What could be so terrible that you'd give up such a cushioned life?"

"I… I saw a monster."

"We all do at some point," the woman said, picking at her nails. Anything outside of a castle was probably a horror show to royals like her.

"No," Letta replied sternly, snapping Lumina out of her boredom. The leader's gaze shifted back to the tattered royal. "I saw something I thought only existed in the likes of the tales my mother would tell my sister and me to make us behave. It was a thing of nightmares, a tall, skinny creature with gray skin and glowing red eyes. And it was my husband."

Lumina chuckled. Had she exaggerated so much at this age? "Royal men can be monsters at times."

"You don't understand. It wasn't human until I started walking to it, and… and…"

The woman's eyes narrowed. Walking toward a monster? She had to admit, the girl must have had a stone or two if this was all true and not just some strange fantasy that possessed her. "If it frightened you so, why would you *walk* to it?"

The Princess took another breath. "For some reason, he seemed more frightened of *me*. I don't believe he wanted me to see him like that."

"Interesting," Lumina muttered under her breath. She had heard rumors of the flesh-eating monster that had terrorized the Apasian people for years, but she'd figured it was one of the stories that commoners often made up to avoid admitting they couldn't defend their animals and children from creatures like wolves.

But perhaps this was a different case. She couldn't necessarily call Letta insane as Lumina herself had seen a balaur firsthand, years ago. The very creature that had put her in this position in the first place. Nothing was out of the question after that, she supposed.

Perhaps the Prince was a shifter. That would explain why the Apasian royals tended to isolate themselves from their people, which was truly a strange practice that no other royals had done—at least not to her knowledge since she created the Phoenix.

"So what did it do to you? Is that why your dress is tattered and bloody?" Lumina inquired.

Letta looked down at her clothing, ashamed. "He did nothing, not to me at least. Someone killed him with a crossbow. I think it was his brother—at least, I saw his balcony was the only one with open windows.

"I looked back and the creature shifted back to... normal form... and he told me to run because his brother would come for me, right before dying in my arms. I was frightened. Now I'm wondering if I should have stayed. Maybe he was mad. I've heard dying people sometimes blurt out nonsense."

"I take it this is the first man you've seen die?"

Staring blankly into space, the Princess nodded.

"Look at me, girl." Letta obeyed. "This won't be the last either. You can't go back. I hope you know that."

"So where do I go?" she asked, and Lumina wasn't sure how to answer. Going back was no option. That would compromise the Phoenix and their location. Letta had seen proof of their existence, even if she wasn't aware of what they were. Of course, there was a chance that anyone she told would think her insane. Outsiders who had heard of the Phoenix often dismissed it as a myth made up by lunatics, but Lumina wasn't willing to take that chance, especially with how astute the girl seemed.

"We'll have to figure that out." Lumina walked out of the tent, feeling the girl's confused eyes on her.

THIRTY-FIVE

ANGHEL

Anghel watched his future wife dancing with other men for the maiden's dance and felt nothing. The hall was nice, the girl was pretty, and the music was good, yet he still felt out of place. If he was this old and still couldn't bring himself to enjoy prim and proper affairs like this, what did it say for the life that was to come?

Glancing around, he made sure no one was looking before he ducked out of the room for some fresh air. He strolled through the open halls of the castle and let his feet hit the polished stone floors, circling the central courtyard to make his way to his room. He felt like he was being watched, but he knew anyone he'd care to hide from was at that dance. Besides, everyone's attention had been on the lovely bride-to-be, her thick, dark, done-up hair flying as she was spun around in dance and the bluest eyes he'd ever seen lighting up with laughter.

He turned a corner, walking up the main staircase that bordered the west side of the courtyard. Based on the limited interaction they'd had so far, Atora was a polite, sweet, courteous girl. She was shy toward him but someone who matched him in attractiveness. He could see why his father had set up the marriage. She seemed bred for the position. Perhaps she'd be even better with political affairs than Anghel himself. She definitely had to be, for everyone to be so fond of her.

Yes, she seemed nice enough, and he was getting older— definitely old enough to be married—but it all seemed so sudden, and he felt like his father had thrown him into it with little warning. He didn't know the girl, and worse yet, didn't feel much of a desire to get to know her better.

The Prince ran his fingers on top of the balcony that overlooked the open area below him as he walked through the hall to his chambers. Perhaps he could still be the same independent, adventurous person he'd always been after the wedding.

No. Who was he kidding? It was too risky. Women—especially whores—talked. Notably so if they were sleeping with a King, and adultery was punishable by death in Padaure. It wouldn't be fair to his father, either, to watch his only son follow in the late Queen's footsteps. Besides, irritating his father with his "lack of maturity" was what had gotten him into this situation so quickly in the first place.

Opening the door to his room, he grabbed a cloak and pulled it over his head, slipping out of the castle and into the town with a bag full of gold coins in hand for his one last night of freedom. He would pay one last visit to his favorite house, and he'd be generous.

The thunder seemed almost as if it were emanating from the walls, a stark contrast to the pitter-patter of the rain on the windows. Anghel had never liked storms. They were always too loud and kept him from his usually sound slumber.

Sitting up, the Prince looked around his room with a sigh, his clothes strewn about on the rich rugs that had been a gift from some far-off kingdom decades ago. Even after getting his last fill of whores, he still couldn't find himself to be excited about the wedding tomorrow. The multiple women at the brothel were a nice distraction, but now it *really* sank in how radically his life would change, how much less pleasure it might carry to spend the rest of his days with a girl who was far too innocent, too naïve for a man like him.

His eyes idly traveled around the room, falling on a tall, slender frame, and he started. His breath quickening, he scrambled to light the nearby lamp to get a better look, only to illuminate the face of his brother standing there, leaning stiffly against a wall on the other side of the room. His arms were crossed with his eyes trained on the floor, but his gaze snapped up upon the lighting of the lamp.

Anghel sighed with relief. "You scared the shit out of me. At least knock, damnit."

"Sorry," Jasper replied softly, in a voice more gravelly than usual. His brows furrowed with a look of confusion flashing across his face.

"What're you doing here, anyways? Come to wish me good luck on my last night as a free man?" He chuckled, and Jasper's humorless eyes rose to meet his. Something was off. His brother was the more serious of the two of them, yes, but this time he didn't even entreat the Prince to an eye roll.

Anghel swallowed nervously. "What's wrong?"

Jasper uncrossed his arms, taking a breath and moving closer. "You're not worthy of her."

"Of who? The girl?"

"Do you even know her *name*?" Jasper scoffed, hollow and cold. "Pathetic, though I'm sure you know the names of all the whores in town."

Anghel rolled his eyes, waving a dismissive hand. "To be fair, I am very well-acquainted with those women. The girl—I only met her a few hours ago. Can you blame me for blanking on her name for a moment? Why do you care so much? Have you even met her yourself?"

"You're *marrying* her tomorrow!" he exclaimed.

"You know I only found out about this the other night, so excuse me for being a bit out of touch with the situation, Jasper."

His brother froze, a brief look of confusion on his face that disappeared so quickly Anghel almost thought it was a figment of his imagination. The Lieutenant's scowl deepened. "The situation," he repeated softly, scoffing and shaking his head before moving closer. Another flash of lightning came up and illuminated the room, as well as his eyes, for just an instant. Had they always been so green? And what was with that large blotch of darkened skin that now seemed to cover his neck?

Jasper stood over him, a shadow enveloping him, and Anghel's uneasiness increased as he saw the man reach behind him while taking a deep breath. "This'll be a lot easier for both of us if you just *stay calm.*"

And with those words, Anghel felt his heart rate slow as a strange wave of peace washed over him, even as he saw his brother pull out the knife. He looked back up in those bright green eyes, and as the blade twisted through his gut with the clap of the thunder, the initial pain started to diminish too. That same tranquil feeling took over, almost as if his emotions were being washed away by some strange force. But the calm didn't stop him from realizing one thing.

This wasn't Jasper.

THIRTY-SIX

JASPER

———

Jasper woke to his friend Osbert shaking him, the sunlight from the pulled-back curtains pouring into the room and blinding him. "Wake up, Lieuten't," he cried frantically. "Somethin's happ'n'd."

"Osbert?" he asked, groggily rubbing the sleep from his eyes. "What're you doing here?"

"It's Anghel."

Jasper sat up with a big yawn. "What'd he do now?"

Osbert swallowed. "It's more 'f... what someone did to him..."

The Lieutenant scoffed. "I don't need to be woken up for boys' talk."

But the Sergeant's eyes were serious. Jasper gave his friend a puzzled look and then shot up hastily, making his way through the door and down the hallway into the other room. As he stopped in his tracks at the scene, his entire body went rigid and his heart dropped.

There lay his brother, a blank look in his wide-open eyes, sitting up against the headboard of his bed. A large splotch of blood on his abdomen stained his clothing and had spread through the bed, soaking the quilt and sheets as well. Jasper rushed over, grabbing his arm and shaking him. "Anghel," he said, his breath catching in his throat and his voice cracking as he tried to hold back a sob. He wished it were some sick joke, but looking at the wound made it all too real. He looked at his brother's face, unable to take his eyes off of the sight. Minutes passed before it sank in, and he wondered who would have done such a thing. He noticed there was no evident fear or shock on the Prince's face. Why did he look so at-peace, so emotionless? While Jasper had seen the bodies of murdered men before, the faces were never so tranquil. Was this a suicide? That wouldn't make sense. Jasper looked around and couldn't see anything nearby that could've been used to create such a wound, and no bloody trail to show that he'd walked away from anything. No, this happened here, in his bed, and by someone he knew.

"My son!" Jasper heard a croak and turned to see Miran, grief-stricken and pulling his hair so strongly that Jasper was surprised it wasn't being torn out. The King rushed over to his side, kneeling beside his son's body. The Lieutenant reached tentatively to put a hand on his shoulder. He'd never seen the King react so emotionally, and Jasper had a hard time dealing with his own shock. But Miran didn't even seem to notice, taking Anghel's hands in his own instead and choking on sobs. "Who would do this?" he wailed.

Jasper himself was speechless. Yes, he was a rascal and a womanizer, but Anghel was a charming man with a good heart deep down. Despite his antics, no one in the castle would wish such a thing upon the Prince, at least as far as he knew.

"I don't know," Jasper said under his breath, only loudly enough for the King to hear. Then he squeezed his adoptive father's shoulder. Turning him, the Lieutenant brought his father into an embrace, trying to hold back his own tears. "But we'll find out."

As they pulled back, Osbert walked over and tapped Jasper on the shoulder, silently beckoning him over to the hallway. The King didn't seem to notice—he had gone back to holding his son's hand in his while bowing his head, his sobs turning into silent shakes. He muttered things under his breath as if he were sharing a word with his son.

"Do you have any clue who might have done this?" Jasper asked in a hushed tone as soon as they'd gotten in the hall, trying not to let their voices carry over.

Osbert hesitated, running a hand through his red hair. "I have me suspicions, sir, but yer' not gonna like 'em."

"This is my *brother*," he spat. "There's nothing about this situation I *like*."

The Sergeant took a deep breath. "We also noticed someone's disappeared."

"Who was it? The Princess? Her servant?" Had Miran told Jasper before deciding, he would have advised him against being so rash with the wedding.

"No, they're still 'ere," he breathed out. "They don' know yet, but I reck'n they'll find out soon."

"Then who would it be?"

"Think, Lieuten't. Rumors fly, an' we all know by now wha' yer brother tried to do to ya, in fron' of a certain lady."

Jasper's jaw tensed up, his eyebrows furrowing and fists clenching. "Careful now."

Osbert threw his hands up. "It's my guess."

"That's not possible."

"If it ain't, why's 'er room empty?"

"You went in her *room*?"

"We knocked first and then found the door unlocked. Ev'rythin's gone, like she wasn' there."

"I don't believe you."

Jasper rushed out of the castle, over to the soldiers' quarters with Osbert on his heels, finding the door to Onyx's room wide open. His friend had been right. The bed was neatly made, the floor swept and everything perfectly placed. The knives and neatly folded clothing she kept around were gone. Had he not known better, he would have thought it had been empty all along.

Jasper gaped at the scene in disbelief. There was not a trace left of her. No note. No clothes. Not even a hair. Had he really scared her off that much last night? He took a deep breath, trying to compose himself. Why would she have disappeared?

"Still don' b'lieve me?"

"She couldn't have done it," he said under his breath.

"She's disappeared the same night yer' brother was *murd'rd*. How do ya think there's no' a link?"

"Because I was with her last night," he confessed.

Osbert went quiet for a moment. "Oh," he murmured. "Though' tha' wa'nt allowed, Lieute'nt."

"Not like *that*." Jasper sighed, sitting on the bed. Burying his head in his hands, he continued, "I apologized about that whole... incident... but something else was wrong, like another thing was on her mind."

"Maybe—"

The Lieutenant shook his head. "No. We skipped the maiden's dance and didn't come back 'til later. It was... quite a talk."

"Oh. Wha' 'bout, if not yer brother?"

Jasper swallowed, unsure if he should continue. Looking around, he took a deep breath. If she really was gone, there was no harm in telling anyone at this point, was there? "How I... feel... about her."

"Hooo," Osbert breathed out, taking a seat by his side with his hands on his knees. "Sorry, Lieute'nt. I din' e'en notice, but I s'pose it makes sense."

Jasper nodded. "I thought it did too."

The Lieutenant found himself seated at a table alongside his Sergeants—Osbert, Tarren, and Bate—as the King walked into the room. His eyes were bloodshot, his hair messier than usual. Jasper had never seen him in such a condition.

"Gentlemen." He nodded, and the men stood up and bowed. None of them seemed to be sure what to make of his voice. On the surface, it sounded calm, but they all knew something was bubbling underneath it. "Have a seat."

Immediately, they obeyed. Miran continued to pace the room languidly, not making eye contact with anyone.

"You all already know of the... incident... that transpired last night," he said coldly, "and it has been brought to my attention that, coincidentally, our newest recruit seems to have disappeared as well. Based on these circumstances, a suspicion has come to my mind that these two events might not be entirely coincidental."

Osbert shot Jasper a look, arching a copper eyebrow as if to say, *Are you going to say something?* Jasper looked back, hesitating. He knew, deep down, that she was innocent, that she wouldn't have done it, no matter how much the Prince annoyed her. But he had to tread lightly. What if she came back? How could he defend her in a way that wouldn't jeopardize the position he'd been working toward all his life as well as the position she held as a valuable soldier?

"And so," the King continued, "I will put an order to avenge my son. If Onyx is spotted by any of you or your men, she is to be killed on sight and the body returned to me as soon as it is done, so I can confirm it."

"Your Majesty," Jasper started, "I would think that to be a bit extreme—"

"*Extreme?*" Miran boomed, turning around with a crazed look in his eyes. An uncomfortable silence filled the room as he slowly walked toward Jasper, placing his hands on the table and leaning in close, his face just inches from the Lieutenant's. "What is *extreme*," he said in a softer voice, "is that the Prince, my only blood, is being embalmed on the day when he was supposed to be *married*. That all my hope for the continuation of my line has been destroyed." His voice steadily grew louder. "That some *bitch*... that I gave a home and occupation... decided to take it for granted and pay me back for it with *this!*"

The Lieutenant swallowed as the King pounded on the table and turned around, pacing the room angrily. Jasper couldn't pretend that his brother's death hadn't been weighing heavily on him or that he didn't understand where Miran was coming from. But it didn't stop him from seeing that the King was not his usual, composed self. He had been replaced with a madman, as if demons had possessed him. Perhaps a parent's grief was its own sort of demon.

"My apologies, Your Majesty," he replied. "I realize that I may have misspoken... all I want is to do right by Anghel. I will personally see to it that we find his killer and bring whoever it is to justice."

Miran turned around. "No, you will not," he said, his voice back to that unstable calm.

Jasper's brows furrowed, and he could feel the Sergeants' eyes on him. "What?"

"You will stay here, with me," the King commanded. "Now that my son is dead, I have no blood heir. I raised you alongside him, and you are the closest thing I have to one. So you will learn from me how to be a King. You will take this lady as your wife, and when the time comes, *you* will take the throne."

The Lieutenant's eyes widened. He'd never considered any rank outside of the Guard, nor did he ever want to be a part of the court, especially not as a Prince or a King. "Sir—"

"That *is* an order, boy," Miran interrupted. "Our Sergeants can take care of the rest." He turned to the other three men. "The first to bring me her body will be promoted to the newly vacant Lieutenant position."

THIRTY-SEVEN

CARNELO

Twirling the wiped knife in his hands, Carnelo sat on a ledge on the outside of the castle, touched only by the rays of moonlight that peeked out from behind the clouds here and there. At first, he'd thought to run away, and he'd made it to the forest before realizing Atora was still there. He decided to wait until nightfall to see her, when he'd have less likelihood of being seen.

He couldn't stop thinking about the night before. He'd killed plenty of animals, hunting for his family and other people in the town and having no problem with it.

But he'd never killed a man before. They were just like animals, sacks of blood and muscle, just as susceptible to blades. Why did it weigh so much on his mind? He had talked himself into going through with it, told himself he was just removing an obstacle to protect Atora before she got hurt. It *had* to be a good solution. Why didn't that thought alone remove the heavy feeling in his chest?

Perhaps it was the name he'd been called. Jasper. He hadn't heard that name in years, not since… He shook his head. It couldn't be. He had wasted no time in fleeing the burnt-down village, but even if he'd never seen his brother's body, there was no chance anyone else had survived. Wouldn't he have figured it out by now? Shaking his head, he told himself the name wasn't necessarily a unique one, and the Prince was probably just delirious, but it didn't shake that eerie feeling.

Looking up, he could see windows above him. The castle here was harder to scale than the one at home because the gaps between the stones were much smaller, so he had to get creative. He was still able to scale up until he found the window leading to Atora, who lay on her bed staring at the ceiling.

He crawled into the room to find her eyes soaked with tears. Turning to him, her eyes lit up with hope, and she jumped up, running to embrace him. "Thank goodness, someone I can talk to," she whispered, her voice a little shaky. "I don't know what you're doing in the Capital, but I'm glad you're still here."

Gently, he held her in his arms, running one of his hands through her hair soothingly. "I'm here," he repeated in a whisper. "Always for you."

They stood there for a few long moments, and he took in that familiar feeling of her small frame leaning into his, her arms wrapped around his waist and her head against his chest. Just this moment alone was more than enough to make the trip to the Capital worth it.

When she pulled back, she sat down on the bed, and he joined by her side, as if they were back in her old bedroom.

"I heard they postponed the wedding," he started.

Atora nodded, staring at the floor and swallowing silently for a moment before she responded. "They found him dead in his bed."

"*What?*" he asked, his tone remaining hushed in case anyone was by her door. He could imagine the security for a

Princess-to-be was quite well set up after a Prince's murder. Carnelo had to pretend to be surprised. He couldn't admit to her what he'd done. She wouldn't understand why he did it, why he *needed* to protect her.

"And the King said something about how I was promised a husband, so I'm going to get married to his brother, though it's not technically his actual brother."

"What do you mean?" He looked at her incredulously with a sinking feeling in his stomach. It hadn't even been a full day since her betrothed passed, and she was already promised to someone else.

She wiped her nose on the sleeve of her nightgown. "Apparently, the Prince has an adoptive brother, some man in charge of the Guard. He wasn't supposed to inherit anything but has to now since the King has no other heir."

"Interesting," he mused. "And have you met him yet? Anything suspicious about him?"

She shook her head. "I wouldn't know. Jasper was apparently busy, so I suppose I'm meeting him tomorrow, after he's finished with whatever it is they do."

Carnelo's stomach twisted into a knot. There was that name again. He hadn't even realized he had been quiet until Atora looked back at him and asked, "What's wrong?"

He shook his head. "I'm... just sorry you have to go through so much."

She laughed hollowly, crossing her ankles and idly tapping her feet on the floor. "I thought getting married was supposed to be easy. That I'd marry a handsome Prince and fall in love and have beautiful children. Now I'm being sent off to someone else like an animal. I guess he's a Prince now, but it feels like marrying a bastard..."

His heart felt like lead. If that's how she felt about royal bastards, how did she feel about a commoner like him? "I imagine it's very hard for you," he whispered, trying not to show his offense.

She looked back up at him, those oblivious eyes looking clear in the little light that seeped in from the window. "It is."

He sighed. "Perhaps an old friend could take your mind off of it," he offered, placing a hand on her shoulder and diminishing the stress she felt. Some tension seemed to fall from her shoulders. "I've heard the plays in the market square are quite entertaining."

She laughed again, this one a little less hollow. "If I manage to sneak out, I think that'd be quite nice."

He gave her a playful half-smile, taking one of her hands in his. "Just wear a cloak, and sneak out through the bridge. I'll find a cart to bring over, and we can look the part of commoners. We'll blend right in, and you can get a break from your worries, just like back home."

Atora smiled. "I would love that."

Climbing out of the window, Carnelo was filled with a new sort of energy. He couldn't pretend he wasn't happy to have at least one more chance with her, and he was determined to make this last one count. When he finished climbing down and landed in the bottom of the small valley that surrounded the castle, he heard faint *thuds* off in the distance, and curiosity got the better of him.

Hiding in the flora as he snuck through, he approached the sounds, careful not to make any noise himself. He peered through the leaves and saw the back of a tall frame, one much like his, quietly grunting as he threw knives at a slab of wood about a dozen yards ahead with only the moonlight to guide him. Carnelo was impressed that the man seemed to be so accurate even in the relative darkness.

As the man walked toward the target and pulled out the blades, Carnelo moved to try to get a good look at his face—and finally did. It was the same as his—the same trace of the angular jawline, the same wavy dark hair, the same nose. Swallowing, it all made sense to him. If it wasn't his imagination playing tricks on him, his twin brother was just fifty feet away with forearms wrapped and blades in his hands.

THIRTY-EIGHT

LUMINA

Lumina rubbed her temples as her top Generals argued over what to do with the Princess.

"She's a loose end. We can just kill 'er—not like anyone'll miss a royal, too many of 'em anyway."

"You've got to be joking. They'll undoubtedly send a search party after her, and that puts the Phoenix at risk."

"Yeah, and the first place they'd look is in the heart of the mountains, *sure!*"

"She's jus' an innocent girl, she din' hurt anyone!"

"Innocent girls've still got big mouths. What'll we do? Send 'er back? That'll just—"

"*Enough!*" Lumina's voice boomed as she placed her hands on the table, leaning over. All of the men and women seated around her went quiet. "I called you here for a discussion," she enunciated, "not for shouting matches and headaches."

A chorus of murmured apologies and under-breath muttering followed before they fell into attentive silence.

"Now that we're all calm, I would like to propose my plan for this situation."

The eyes of ten Generals around the pockmarked table in her tent were trained on their leader, who, despite her short frame, had the presence to hold their attention.

She stood up straight, taking a slow breath before continuing. "It is quite clear that sending her back is not an option. The poor girl will either be locked away, or worse, run her mouth about us. That *could* come back to haunt us, even if there's a small chance of it. But I suppose we might have to change our location anyways, even if she's telling the truth and was able to just stumble upon us."

A few of them nodded and murmured, "Yes," and, "Of course."

"On the other hand," Lumina continued, "that leaves us with the question of where she goes if not back. She might die on her own if we send her to another place. Even if she doesn't, we know some kingdoms are more allied than others, or that some are foes. Either one means she might be recognized, so that is also not an option."

"So we kill 'er then?" asked Amabel, the Inecori General nervously drumming her long and graceful tan fingers on the table.

Lumina shook her head, waiting for the others to catch on to her idea. "Not necessarily."

"You can't seriously consider letting her join us," Tybalt retorted, his bald forehead crinkling. "A *royal*? They're the ones we try to take down!" He waved a hand dismissively. "We can finish the job with her here and be on our way."

She flashed him a glare. "Need I remind you that we found you half-dead in the streets, *Tybalt*, and were kind enough to take you in? If you forgot, we can send you back for a recollection."

Tybalt swallowed and kept his mouth shut, looking down shamefully.

"Likewise, she is healthy, albeit weak, for now. And from what I can read of her, she does have potential. We need all the people we can get, and if she accepts the offer, we train her up like we did the others. With enough tests of loyalty and time in training, she can be just as good as any other scout or informant, possibly even better."

"But what if she doesn't want to? Or if she betrays us?" Amabel mused, her large, curious green eyes trained on her leader.

Lumina gave her a small, malignant smile. "Then we do what we would with any other, of course. Send her on her way and see how far she can get before the arrows hit."

The Generals nodded solemnly.

The leader clasped her hands together, satisfied. "So it's decided."

Borin shrugged. "Sounds good to me, ma'am." Other mumbles of agreement followed, and a bigger smile grew on Lumina's face. If everything went well, they could use the girl's royal background to provide insight, especially on Apasian and Padaurean territories and weaknesses.

"Moving on," she announced, turning to two Generals on her left. "Any birds back from Padaure or the Lebirosi Midstad?"

Aldreda, a General with curly, close-cropped black hair in charge of the Lebiros intelligence, shook her head, her rich dark complexion glowing in the lanternlight. Despite the worry she must have felt, her expression remained composed, a talent of hers in any situation. "We sent a scout there last night, at your order, but the bird hasn't returned yet. We should be hearing back within the next few days."

"What about you, Herry?" Lumina inquired to the man on her left, who had a wolfish, stubbled face with long brown hair tied back in a bun.

He shook his head. "No word back yet, ma'am. You'll know the second I hear something."

The leader nodded, not very much comforted by the thought. Dismissing the council, she paced the room, fiddling with the tiny gold chain around her neck.

THIRTY-NINE

ATORA

———

Atora had followed Zbura's instructions and taken extra precautions. She tied her hair back into a bun and covered her head with a headscarf, in addition to a cloak on top of her simplest dress, before walking through the gates and telling the guards she was just going for a quick walk to get some fresh air. She politely yet firmly declined when they insisted on joining her, and they gave up with a shrug.

Just as she slipped out of their sight, she found, as promised, her old friend on a small cart pulled by two horses with a couple of bags and some hay strewn about in the back. "My apologies for such a shabby ride," he offered. "I realize this is not grand enough for a lady—"

"But it does provide the cover that I would need to go into the town," she finished.

He smiled and nodded, stepping down and lending his hand to help her up onto the seat. "Precisely."

She couldn't lie. It was nice to have a peek at relatively normal life. Although chaos and grief seeped through every corner of the castle, she was shocked to find the commoners going about their lives. They milled about on the cobblestone streets between their scarlet-topped buildings, buying and selling food and clothing and other goods while chatting with one another as if nothing had happened. Were their worlds really so separated?

The play put on was just like the ones she'd sneak out to see at home—boasting silly plotlines with childish jokes—but she enjoyed this guilty pleasure, nonetheless. With all that had happened, it was a more-than-welcome one, especially with her best friend by her side. For at least a little while, everything felt normal, as if she was back home with him. She managed to forget about her troubles, giggling as she watched the men in scraggly rags dance around and insult each other in exaggerated tones.

By the time the play ended, sunset was falling over the kingdom, and she linked her arm through Zbura's as he led her back and helped her up into the cart.

Winding through the streets and alleyways, she leaned back on her forearms, watching the red roofs they passed by and admiring the golden light spilling out of the inns and taverns. She heard laughter and drinking songs while others had houses with little children running in and old women chattering with one another on the benches in front.

"Do people not know, or do they not care?" she wondered aloud.

"I'm sure the old ladies do," he chuckled. "They gossip about everything on those benches. That's often how rumors spread the fastest."

"I'm serious," she insisted.

He sighed, a bit more somber. "They pretend to care for the sake of nobility, but in all reality, the business of royals doesn't usually concern commoners. Most don't see a reason to even think about it unless it involves them."

"But we are their leaders," she protested. "The family in power. The ones that rule over them." Were commoners back home so indifferent to her and her family as well?

"That's true," Zbura admitted, "but again, unless it directly affects a commoner, they don't think about it."

"Is that true for you too?"

He glanced over at her briefly but kept his eyes on the road above and his hands on the reins. "If it were, why would I be here with you?"

"Zbura," she said with a pause, not quite sure how to ask him what was on her mind. He looked at her for a bit longer, cueing her to continue. Taking a deep breath, she asked, "Did you come all this way for me?"

Giving her another sigh, he replied, "I come to the Capital from time to time for my trade. I always make better sales here."

"Oh." Was he just here out of convenience?

"But I would be lying if I said that was the main reason to come this time."

"Why?" she asked, tilting her head curiously.

"I didn't like how we left things," he said with another flick of his wrist on the reins. "I wanted to ensure you were alright. That you were being taken care of. That…"

"That what?"

"That I could see you again. One more time."

"Oh." She admittedly hadn't given much thought to what it would mean for her friendship with him for her to move leagues away from home. Would this be their last interaction? It couldn't be. Could it?

Maybe it was. She wasn't sure how the royal family would feel about her sneaking out to the city to befriend a commoner on the occasional trip over, especially since her father hadn't been fond of the idea. But if the Prince had been friends with soldiers, this shouldn't be any different. Unless the standards here were different for a Princess.

"Then certain events transpired. I decided to stick around to keep an eye on everything. I swore I would keep you safe," he continued. "You're important to me, and I wouldn't be able to forgive myself if anything happened to you."

She observed his face in the fading light. His beautiful green eyes focused straight ahead on the road, and a breeze blew his wavy dark hair out of his face. Her gaze trailed down to his toned forearms and rough hands that gripped the reins tightly enough that his knuckles turned white.

"I appreciate that," she finally said. Any anxiety she had rising up suddenly fell away in his otherwise calm presence. "And I *am* glad you're here. I know I'm safe now."

"That's all I want for you," he said, meeting her eyes again for an instant before focusing on the road. "To be safe and happy."

She nodded, giving him a half-hearted smile, but he seemed too focused on the road ahead to look at her. As nice as her Prince had seemed, she wondered if he would ever have said something like that to her. Or if her new betrothed would.

Following Zbura's gaze, she saw dirt roads stretching ahead, off into the distance, and green fields surrounding them, peppered with hay bales that grew sparser the farther out they went. It wasn't often she saw sights like this.

But why was she seeing them? Looking back, she spotted the city behind them as she grew groggier. Only as her eyes closed and she started drifting off did she realize, with a surprising amount of peace, that he wasn't taking her back to the castle.

FORTY

———

She sprinted down the path leading into her friend's clay cottage in the early rays of dawn to find Jade lying in her bed, trying to cover her wails with winces and whimpers. Ignoring the soaked bed, she knelt to hold Jade's hand and received a squeeze so tight she wondered where that strength had come from, almost as if her friend's pain was being transferred through to her.

But it didn't matter. What did was that Jade was here with the people she loved the most: her best friend and her husband, who ran around the house to bring her what she needed while the village midwife pleaded with her to keep pushing.

"Look at me," the blonde woman told the one in labor, meeting those granite eyes. "You'll be all right after this. Just keep pushing." She couldn't pretend to understand the pain Jade was going through. But looking into each other's eyes seemed to give her a bit more strength, and the mother nodded with a sense of resolve as she winced again.

It felt like hours passed by, and she couldn't help but wonder where Jade's willpower came from, to keep pushing through the excruciating pain that she must have been in. She was so focused on her friend and her struggles that she barely noticed the mess that the midwife gently guided out. Finally, Jade took one large, deep breath, her tired eyes filling up with a new sort of life and energy. She followed her friend's gaze to see the midwife gently carrying the newborn over.

The new mother's arms reached out to hold the child in her arms, happy tears welling up in her eyes. Chryso had just walked in with more water for his wife and rushed over, placing the cup on the tiny table by the bed. He leaned over and looked at the child, his eyes happily watering as it wailed, protesting when the midwife came over to pick it up. But eventually, he let her go and followed the woman closely behind as she went into the other room to wash the infant.

"You did it," the blonde woman whispered, joyfully tearing up herself and looking at her friend with pride.

Jade turned her head, tears streaking down her face, a strange contrast with the large grin on her face. "With you two by my side, I can do anything."

She leaned over and gave the mother a kiss on the forehead. "Always here for you."

"And I'd like you to be the godmother."

She couldn't help but match her friend's beam, a tear rolling down her cheek as she gently squeezed her friend's hand. "Of course."

They were interrupted by Chryso walking in, his firm arms holding the child ever so gently. It had calmed down, and its thick hair was now more visible. The man gently transferred the child into Jade's arms, giving his wife a long, lingering kiss on the head. "It's a girl," he whispered.

"Oh!" Jade exclaimed, a tear trailing down her cheek. "She's absolutely beautiful."

"Only because she has her mother's eyes," he commented, and Jade's beaming smile grew even wider than before.

"What's her name?" the godmother asked the couple.

They looked at her, puzzled. "We hadn't decided on that," Jade admitted, ever so gently brushing the child's hair with her fingers. "We weren't sure what would be a good name, and now, looking at her, I'm at a loss for words."

"You'll figure it out," she replied. They nodded, and silence followed.

After a bit of time passed, Jade broke it. "Would you like to hold her?" she offered.

The blonde woman hesitated. Never before had she held a baby, she realized, especially not a newborn one. But this was the child of her two closest friends, a child she already loved and knew she would only grow to love more as time went on.

Nodding, she gently lifted the child out of the mother's arms and into her own. The baby girl looked back up at her, with large eyes—dark gray with specks of hazel and white, just like her mother's.

Softly, she patted the fine hairs on the child's head, a beautiful dark gold. "She really does have your eyes," she gushed, "and her father's hair—almost the color of citrine."

Another silence followed, and she looked back up to see the couple glancing between themselves and then back at her.

Jade was the first to break it, that grin still on her face. "We'll call her Citrina, then."

ACKNOWLEDGMENTS

———

To all of the family and friends who have made this possible, thank you so much! I want to especially thank those who have encouraged me along the way, who have supported me through the process of writing and publishing this story, and for those who continue to encourage me as I write more content for the future!

To my parents and closest friends, Delia and Claudiu Popoviciu, I cannot thank you enough for the endless support you've always given me in every area of my life, and especially in my writing, even when I was a little girl scribbling story ideas in notebooks. You have given me so much, in love, in uplifting me, and in bringing me to a country with endless opportunities while making sure I never forgot who I was or where I came from, doing your best in guiding me throughout my life to be the best version of myself that I can be.

To my brother, Victor—for being one of my best friends and among my favorite people to talk to. Words cannot describe how much you mean to me and how proud I am of the person and man you're becoming, and who you have yet to be.

Thank you to my grandparents—Eugenia and Octavian Popoviciu, and Verona and Teodor Mălan—who have passed their stories and the stories of our ancestors down to me. You have encouraged me in my goals and in the life I've built, even from the other side of the world. Thank you also for reminding me to never forget my Romanian heritage. I haven't, and it's a beautiful part of me that I look to continue sharing with the world.

To Florica Mindea and the Mindea family for giving me and my family a home when we felt so far from our own. We are eternally grateful for how you've uplifted us, as a mentor, as a woman, and as one of the greatest friends we've had. My family and I would not be anywhere near where we are now without your help.

I would also like to thank Eric Koester, Brian Bies, Amanda Munro, Faiqa Zafar, and the entire team at New Degree Press, who have taken a chance on me and guided me as a new author through every part of the process. You have done the most to develop my work into something better than I could have imagined creating.

To one of my closest friends, Bradley Moyer—thank you for always being there for me and supporting me on this journey since day one. I'm incredibly thankful for your friendship, for keeping me accountable as a person, and for the time you've taken to help me in reading and editing my content as well.

Thank you also to Nicholas, who has not only helped me in brainstorming, worldbuilding, and beta reading, but also in being there for me and supporting me every step of the way, celebrating every milestone I've hit, both large and small—even when I was too tired to recognize it myself.

To my beta readers—Emma Gurchiek, Jorge Huete, Bradley Moyer, Jordyn Musi, Leah Pickner, Shreya Ramesh, Alice Shashkina, Sabrina Sukhin, Andrew Whiteman, and Polina Yagusevich—thank you as well. I greatly appreciate you all as my friends and for the kindness you showed me in taking the time to read my work and helping me refine it to what it is today, in addition to the support you've given me along the way.

I would like to thank the community of people who have helped me in this journey, not only in spirit but also in pre-ordering my book so I could raise the money to make this happen in the first place: Megan Agresta, Radu Almasan and the Almasan family, the Arnold family, Adelina and Marius Balog, Daniela Barbolovici, Tara Batchik, Kaitlynn Bauman, Austin Bean, the Blum family, Leslie Brown, Benjamin Browngardt and the Browngardt family, Matthew Butcher, Harine Choi, Ioana Cirstescu, Glenn Clune, Tyler Cowans, the Dragos family, Sebastian and Liana Dragu, Gianni Fatica, Michele Garry, the German family, David Girbino, the Giurgiu family, Alaina Graziano, Cristina Haidau, Robert Hammitt, Ryan Harty, Jacob Holfeltz, Denisa Ilea, the Ionescu family, Jeesoo Kim, Kyle Kinkopf, Celia Kusmer, John LaGue, the Lazuran family, Keith Luria, Gabriel Madonna, Marius Malan, Pam Markt, Michael Medina, Max Mirho, Joseph and Doina Moldovan, Nancy Monro, the Naghiu family, Ana Nedelcu, Father Ian and Mary Lynn Pac-Urar, Tomas Padegimas, Michael Pawlusik, Josh Pickner and the Pickner family, the Pod family, Puiu and Mariana Popoviciu, Becky

Poszywak, Nicoleta Radu, the Rollins family, the Rosca family, Gheorghe Salajan, the Segall family, Gent Semaj, Alexandra Sidor, Brandon Slaght, the Stanulet family, the Tira family, Alina Tirlea, Emily Waterhouse, Caitlin Whichello, the Whiteman family, Allison Wood, and Nika Zaslavsky. I am so thankful for you all, and it means the world to me to have so many people in my life helping me achieve a longtime dream of mine that I am happy to now call a reality.

Finally, I would like to thank God for His guidance and providing me the opportunity to grow up in and integrate the cultures of two wonderful countries, for the life experiences He has given to me and my family that have inspired me in my work, and for the endless blessings He continues to give to me in terms of the people He has put in my life and the opportunities that have been put in my path.

Made in the USA
Columbia, SC
09 May 2021